USDA

United States
Department of
Agriculture

Forest Service

Northern Research
Station

General Technical
Report NRS-P-10

Proceedings
17th U.S. Department of Agriculture Interagency Research Forum on Gypsy Moth and Other Invasive Species, 2006

THE NORTHERN LIMIT
OF YOUR RANGE:
40°45 N   41°N
42°N LATITUDE
(and still expanding!)

ACKNOWLEDGMENTS

Thanks go to Vincent D'Amico for providing the cover artwork, "The Northern Limit".

Proceedings
17th U.S. Department of Agriculture
Interagency Research Forum on
Gypsy Moth and Other
Invasive Species, 2006

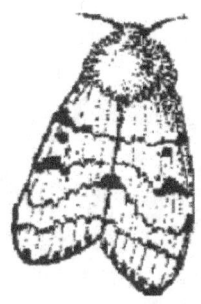

January 10-13, 2006
Loews Annapolis Hotel
Annapolis, Maryland

Edited by
Kurt W. Gottschalk

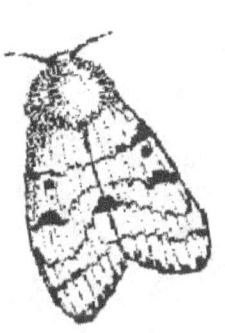

Sponsored by:

Forest Service Research

Agricultural Research Service

Animal and Plant Health Inspection Service

Cooperative State Research, Education and Extension Service

USDA

CONTENTS

FOREWORD

This meeting was the 17th in a series of annual USDA Interagency Gypsy Moth Research Forums that are sponsored by the USDA Gypsy Moth Research and Development Coordinating Group. The title of this year's forum reflects the inclusion of other invasive species in addition to gypsy moth. The Committee's original goal of fostering communication and an overview of ongoing research has been continued and accomplished in this meeting.

The proceedings document the efforts of many individuals: those who made the meeting possible, those who made presentations, and those who compiled and edited the proceedings. But more than that, the proceedings illustrate the depth and breadth of studies being supported by the agencies and it is satisfying, indeed, that all of this can be accomplished in a cooperative spirit.

USDA Gypsy Moth Research and Development Coordinating Group

Kevin Hackett, Agricultural Research Service (ARS)
Vic Mastro, Animal and Plant Health Inspection Service (APHIS)
Bob Nowierski, Cooperative State Research, Education and Extension Service (CSREES)
Robert Bridges, Forest Service-Research (FS-R), Chairperson

Acknowledgments

The program committee would like to thank Hercon Environmental, Arborjet, Inc., JJ Mauget Company, and the Management and Staff of the Loews Annapolis Hotel for their support of this meeting.

Program Committee:

Mike McManus, Kevin Thorpe, Vic Mastro, Joseph Elkinton, and Barbara Johnson

Local Arrangements:

Kathleen Shields, Katherine McManus

Proceedings Publication:

Kurt Gottschalk

JAPANESE OAK WILT AS A NEWLY EMERGED FOREST PEST IN JAPAN: WHY DOES A SYMBIOTIC AMBROSIA FUNGUS KILL HOST TREES?"

Naoto Kamata[1], Koujiro Esaki[2], Kenryu Kato[1], Hisahito Oana[1], Yutaka Igeta[1] and Ryotaro Komura[1]

[1]Graduate School of Natural Science and Technology, Kanazawa University, Kakuma, Kanazawa, Ishikawa 920-1192, Japan

[2]Ishikawa Forest Experiment Station, Tsurugi, Ishikawa 920-2114

ABSTRACT

Japanese oak wilt (JOW) has been known since the 1930s, but in the last 15 years epidemics have intensified and spread to the island's western coastal areas. The symbiotic ambrosia fungus *Raffaelea quercivora* is the causal agent of oak dieback, and is vectored by *Platypus quercivorus* (Murayama). This is the first example of an ambrosia beetle fungus that kills vigorous trees. Mortality of *Quercus crispula* Blume was approximately 40 percent but much lower for associated species of Fagaceae, even though each species had a similar number of beetle attacks. It is likely that other oaks resistant to the fungus evolved under a stable relationship between the tree, fungus and beetle during a long evolutionary process. *Quercus crispula* was probably not part of this coevolution. This hypothesis was supported by the fact that *P. quercivorus* showed the least preference for *Q. crispula*, yet exhibited highest reproductive success in this species (The index of an increasing rate = ca. 4). On contrary, on the other oaks the index was almost one that guarantees a stable population dynamics for *P. quercivorus*. Therefore, *P. quercivorus* could spread more rapidly in stands with a high composition of *Q.crispula*. Each of individual trees other than *Q. crispula* can be utilized by *P. quercivorus* for several years. On contrary, *P. quercivorus* can reproduce only one year on each *Q. crispula* tree because necrosis of sapwood tissues spread widely after the first-year attack. The relationship among *Q. crispula—R. quercivora—P. quercivorus* seems evolutionary unstable. JOW seems to be an invasive pest of *Q. crispula*. Concentric patterns of JOW spread also support this hypothesis.

Introduction

Since the late 1980s, Japanese oak wilt (JOW) has been prevalent in Japan (Ito and Yamada 1998). JOW has been recorded since the 1930s, but up to 1980, epidemics lasted for only a few years and were confined to a few areas on the west side of Japan. More recently, epidemics have lasted for more than 15 years, and the area of JOW has been spreading to new localities where JOW has never been recorded in the past. These incidences of oak dieback have tended to spread concentrically from a source population (Kamata et al. 2002), exhibiting a pattern of spread typical of introduced invasive species. *Raffaelea quercivora* was proved to be implicated in JOW by inoculation experiment of the fungus (Ito et al. 1998). The ambrosia beetle, *Platypus quercivorus* (Murayama) (Coleoptera: Platypodidae), is a major vector of this fungus (Ito et al. 1998), because (1) affected dead trees are almost always infested by this species; (2) the fungus is found frequently in gallery systems of *P. quercivorus*; and (3) the fungus also occurs inside the beetle's mycangia, in which the fungus is carried to a new host tree.

Ambrosia beetles usually attack weakened or dead trees. The present case in Japan is the first example of an ambrosia fungus carried by an ambrosia beetle that kills vigorous trees. *Platypus quercivorus* can reproduce regardless of host fate following the insect attack. Necrosis has been observed around the gallery systems in sapwood, and has been attributed to *R. quercivora* (Ito and Yamada 1998). The necrosis stops water conductance, and a tree dies when necrosis completely blocks any cross section of the tree (Kuroda and Yamada 1996).

Life history of *P. quercivorus*

Platypus quercivorus is basically univoltine in Japan with an occasional second generation (Sone et al. 1998). Adult emergence of the main overwintering generation was observed from May to September with a peak in early July, and emergence of the second generation has been observed from late August to early December. Dispersal flight of the newly eclosed adults detected by sticky interception traps continued from late June to early December with a peak in July and early August (Esaki et al. 2004). After a male selects a tree for a breeding site, it initially bores a cylindrical entrance hole about 15 mm in extent into the tree. When a female arrives later at the entrance, the male emerges from the entrance and leads the female into the tunnel. After mating at the entrance hole, the male follows the female into the tunnel and she starts to bore a horizontal gallery. A male and female pair reproduce in one galley. On the thorax, a female has a mycangia, in which it carries spores of symbiotic ambrosia fungi. The female lays eggs on the walls of the gallery, inoculating spores of the ambrosia fungi on the wall of the galley. The female grazes on the ambrosia fungi to continue to lay eggs by the end of autumn (mid-November in Ishikawa). The parents were supposed to die before or during the winter because no eggs were found in the spring. The eggs hatch within about a week, and the larvae grazed on the ambrosia fungi covering the walls of the horizontal galley. Larvae pass through five instars. Matured larvae formed pupal cradles vertically and pupated in these cradles. Individuals that could pupate by the autumn (mid-October in Ishikawa) emerge as adults of the second generation. The others overwinter as a larval stage and pupate in the following season.

Preference-performance relationship of *P. quercivorus* among different oak species

Although 45 species among 27 genera in 17 families of woody plants have been recorded as host plants of *P. quercivorus*, woody plants belonging to the Fagaceae are considered as essential hosts of *P. quercivorus* because beetle attack density is significantly higher on trees in this family. There are many records of *P. quercivorus* outbreaks in stands of evergreen species of Fagaceae in Japan, but few evergreen trees have been killed by this ambrosia beetle fungus even though many entry holes have been found on the trunk surface. In Ishikawa, the mortality of newly attacked *Q. crispula* was ca. 40 percent, but low mortality was observed in associated species of Fagaceae (Kamata et al. 2002). However, the numbers of new entry holes made by this beetle in different species of Quercus were similar. Several studies also proved that *Q. crispula* was much more susceptible to this fungus than other sympatric species of Fagaceae.

The reproductive success of *P. quercivorus* differed among the four species of Fagaceae: *Q. crispula* was the most suitable host species for reproduction (mean no. of offspring adults emerged per gallery = ca. 8), while the number was almost two for *Q. serrata*, *Q. acuta*, and *Castanopsis cuspidata* (Kato et al. 2001). *Platypus quercivorus* failed to reproduce in *Q. crispula* and *Q. serrata* trees that had been infested in the previous year. In the second year of this insect attack, adults of *P. quercivorus* avoided the necrosis of sapwood when they tunneled. The advancing necrosis caused by *R. quercivora* was then likely to make the tree less suitable as a substrate for ambrosia fungi and/or for *P. quercivorus*. Hydrolyzable tannin contained in healthy sapwood was converted to ellagic acid and gallic acid by *R. quercivora* tannase (Kasai et al. 2003). Purprogallincarboxylic acid was bio-converted with *R. quercivora* laccase from gallic acid. Hence great amount of ellagic acid (0.05% w/wet weight) and small of gallic acid (0.001% w/wet weight) was contained in discolored necrosis of sapwood (Oana et al. 2003). Adults of *P. quercivorus* avoid these tannic acids in discolored necrosis.

The rate of development of the necrosis is a key to determining tree mortality following *P. quercivorus* attack and reproductive success of this insect in the second year attack and thereafter. Because it was slow by comparison in evergreen species of Fagaceae, these trees are less susceptible to *R. quercivora* than *Q. crispula* and *P. quercivorus* can reproduce on these in the second year attack.

In a stand with a low percentage of *Q. crispula*, *P. quercivorus* showed the least preference for *Q. crispula* (Kamata et al. 2002), although its reproductive success was highest on this species. An inverse relationship was found between the preference of *P. quercivorus* for different tree species and its performance on these species. Its greatest preference was for *Castanopsis sieboldii* (Fagaceae) with 45.6 percent and 67.6 percent of trees attacked in 1999 and 2000, respectively. Because reproductive success of *P. quercivorus* on trees other than *Q. crispula* is low, aerial population density of P. *quercivorus* adults in this stand (L) was lower than in the other stand with a high percentage of *Q. crispula* (H) (H/L=45.8 in 1999, 3.3 in 2000). The percentage mortality of *Q. crispula* was low in this stand and the tree composition of the stand was stable. In the stand with a high percentage of *Q. crispula*, in contrary, infestation spreads out very rapidly on every Fagaceae trees. Tree mortality of newly infested Q. crispula was about 40 percent every year, which caused great changes in tree composition.

Thus, the oak *Q. cripsula* was preferred least by *P. quercivorus*, but it was the most suitable host for reproduction and was susceptible to the symbiotic ambrosia fungus. The relationship among *Q. crispula*—*R. quercivora*—*P. quercivorus* seems evolutionary unstable. It is likely that other oaks resistant to the fungus evolved under a stable relationship between the tree, fungus and beetle during a long evolutionary process. *Quercus crispula* was probably not part of this coevolution. JOW seems an invasive pest of *Q. crispula*. JOW occurs in the northern regions and high elevation margins of the distribution of *P. quercivorus* and on the southern / low elevation margins of the distribution of *Q. crispula*. JOW epidemic in Japan probably resulted from the warmer climate that occurred from the late 1980s, which made possible the fateful encounter of *P. quercivorus* with *Q. cripsula* by allowing the beetle to extend its distribution to more northerly latitudes and higher elevations (Kamata et al. 2002).

Literature Cited

Esaki, K.; Kato, K.; Kamata, N. 2004. **Stand-level distribution and movement of *P. quercivorus* adults and patterns of incidence of new Infestation**. Agricultural and Forest Entomology 6:1-11.

Ito, S.; Kubono, T.; Sahashi, N.; Yamada, T. 1998. **Associated fungi with the mass mortality of oak trees**. J. Jpn. For. Soc. 80: 170-175.

Ito, S.; Yamada, T. 1998. **Distribution and spread of mass mortality of oak trees**. J. Jpn. For. Soc. 80: 229-232.

Kamata, N.; Esaki, K.; Kato, K.; Igeta, Y.; Wada, K. 2002. **Impact of global warming on deciduous oak dieback caused by ambrosia fungus carried by ambrosia beetle in Japan**. Bull. Entomol. Res. 92: 119-126.

Kasai, M.; Mitsunaga, T.; Ito, S.; Kamata, N. 2003. **Study of *Quercus mongolica* wood extractives damaged from *Platypus quercivorous* attack II. -Denaturalization of a hydrolyzable tannin by *Raffaelea quercivora*-**. Abstracts Annual Meeting of the Japan Wood Research Society (Web Version) 53:

Kato, K.; Esaki, K.; Igeta, Y.; Kamata, N. 2001. **Preliminary report on comparison of reproductive success of *Platypus quercivorus* among four species of the family Fagaceae**. Chubu Forest Research 49: 81-84.

Kuroda, K.; Yamada, T. 1996. **Discoloration of sapwood and blockage xylem sap ascent in the trunks of wilting *Quercus* spp. following attack by *Platyous quercivorus***. Journal of the Japanese Forestry Society 78: 84-88.

Oana, H.; Kakiuchi, N.; Esaki, K.; Kasai, M.; Mitsunaga, T.; Ito, S.; Mikage, M.; Kamata, N. 2003. **Comparison of chemical composition of xylem extract between healthy sapwood and necrosis caused by an ambrosia beetle *Platypus quercivorus* (Murayama)(Coleoptera: Platypodidae) the previous year**. Chubu Forest Research 51: 189-190.

Sone, K.; Mori, T.; Ide, M. 1998. **Life history of the oak borer, *Platypus quercivorus* (Murayama) (Coleoptera: Platypodidae)**. Applied Entomology and Zoology 33: 67-75.

TOWARD THE DEVELOPMENT OF SURVEY TRAPPING TECHNOLOGY FOR THE EMERALD ASH BORER

Therese Poland[1], Damon Crook[2], Joseph Francese[2], Jason Oliver[3],
Gard Otis[4], Peter de Groot[5], Gary Grant[5], Linda MacDonald[5],
Deborah McCullough[6], Ivich Fraser[2], David Lance[2], Victor Mastro[2],
Nadeer Youssef[2], Tanya Turk[4], Melodie Youngs[4]

[1]USDA Forest Service, North Central Research Station, 1407 S. Harrison Rd., Rm. 220,
E. Lansing, MI 48823

[2]USDA APHIS PPQ, Otis Pest Survey, Detection and Exclusion Laboratory, Bldg. 1398 W. Truck Rd., Otis
ANGB, MA 02542

[3]Tennessee State University, Nursery Crop Research Station, 472 Cadillac Lane, McMinnville, TN 37110

[4]Department of Environmental Biology, University of Guelph, Guelph,
Ontario, Canada N1G 2W1

[5]Canadian Forest Service, Great Lakes Forestry Centre, 1219 Queen St. E.,
Sault Ste. Marie, Ontario, Canada P6A 5M7

[6]Department of Entomology, Michigan State University, E. Lansing, MI 48824

ABSTRACT

Improved survey tools are essential for accurately delimiting the infestation of emerald ash borer (EAB), *Agrilus planipennis* Fairmaire (Coleoptera: Buprestidae) and for detecting new infestations. Current survey methods including visual surveys for damage, girdled trap trees, and trunk dissections are less than ideal because newly infested trees typically do not display external symptoms and trap trees and trunk dissections are destructive and labor intensive. Here we present a summary of research conducted by scientists from several organizations on the development of efficacious trapping techniques for *A. planipennis*. Studies included the identification of host attractants and testing responses by *A. planipennis* in the laboratory, field trapping experiments evaluating different trap designs and baits, and trap tree studies comparing girdling, baiting, and different colored bands.

Ash leaf extracts were prepared and volatiles were collected from girdled and healthy ash trees. Volatile components were screened for *A. planipennis* antennal activity using coupled gas chromatographic electro-antennal detection (GC-(GC-EAD) in the USDA APHIS and CFS laboratories. Several antenally-active compounds were identified. Volatile compounds were tested using *A. planipennis* adults in a two-choice walking olfactomter bioassay in the USDA Forest Service laboratory. Significant attractive responses were found to green ash leaf extract, nonanal, pentadecane, trans-2-hexenol, and trans-caryophyllene.

Field trapping experiments conducted by USDA APHIS and Tennessee State University compared different colors, trap designs, and trap placement. A four panel 'hanging box' design made of corrugated plastic coated with Pestick insect glue was used to test four colors simultaneously. Colors tested included black, yellow, white, purple, red, green, navy and silver. More beetles were caught on purple traps than any other color. In another study 19 colors were tested including colors produced by the plastic manufacturer, purple-colored glue, glue containing small green or purple metallic objects, metallic foils, and paints reflecting in the 400-450 nm range. Purple-colored glue caught the most beetles followed by glue mixed with green glitter, and the manufacturer's purple. In the trap design experiment, several sizes, shapes and colors were tested. Most traps were made from purple or black corrugated plastic covered in Pestick insect glue. The Lindgren funnel trap and IPM Tech Intercept Panel trap (both black-colored), a new purple-colored elm bark beetle trap placed around a host tree, and girdled trap trees were also tested. Girdled trap trees were significantly more attractive than any of the trap designs. The purple elm bark beetle traps placed around host trees were more attractive than any other trap design except for the large purple panel 'prototype' traps. Traps with larger surface areas were the most effective. The Lindgren funnel trap, the IPM Tech Panel trap and another black-colored corrugated plastic trap caught no EAB. To test trap location, traps composed of two Pestick-coated purple corrugated plastic strips were placed along the edge of a woodlot, 25 m into the woods, or 25 m from the woodlot in an open field. On two dates, the number of beetles captured was significantly greater on traps located along the forest edge compared to traps in the open field or woods. No beetles were captured on traps in the woods. In a field trapping experiment conducted by University of Guelph traps that employed various patterns of purple and magenta were compared including stripes, ovals and metallic ovals. There was a slight discrimination between different patterns with magenta and green patterns being more attractive than magenta alone or green alone; striped patterns catured more beetles than oval patterns; and metallic ovals were more attractive than nonmetallic ovals. The USDA Forest Service, CFS, and MSU compared baited and unbaited traps and traps of different shapes. Purple panel 'prototype' traps baited with a blend of host volatiles (α-humulene, pentadecane, trans-3-hexenol, and trans-caryophyllene) captured significantly more beetles than traps baited with individual compounds. Cross vane, triangular, and flat purple corrugated plastic traps baited with a blend of host volatiles (hexanal, trans-2-hexenol, and cis-3-hexenol) captured significantly more beetles than unbaited traps.

Several trap tree studies were conducted by USDA APHIS, USDA FS, MSU, University of Guelph, and CFS comparing girdled or healthy trap trees with different colored bands. Colored bands did not increase attraction to trap trees in any of the studies. USDA APHIS and Tennessee State University tested attraction of A. planipennis to green ash nursery trees of three varieties ('cimmaron', 'patmore', and 'urbanite') that were injured by crown decapitation, trunk scraping, root pruning, or girdling. The number of beetles captured did not differ significantly between treatments but there was a trend toward higher catches on girdle and trunk-scraped trees and on the 'urbanite' variety. A trap tree study conducted by CFS found that open-grown trap trees captured significantly more A. planipennis than trap trees located in a closed canopy stand. The number of beetles captured on trap trees along the edge of a stand was intermediate. The USDA FS and MSU compared healthy trap trees and trap trees that were girdled by removing a 6"-wide band of bark, wounded by removing a vertical strip of bark with the same dimensions as the horizontal girdle, or stressed by spraying the bark of the lower 1.5-m section of the bole to run-off with the herbicide, Garlon-4. Significantly more A. planipennis adults were captured on the trees stressed with herbicide than the healthy trap trees. Captures on girdled trees or trees with a vertical wound were intermediate. Trap trees were felled and completely peeled during the fall. The density of larval galleries was significantly higher in girdled trees compared to healthy trees or trees stressed with herbicide. The number captured on trees with vertical wounds was intermediate. Although trees stressed with herbicide captured more adults and appeared to be more attractive initially, they died very quickly, and thus may not have been suitable for subsequent attacks and larval development. Overall, girdled trap trees are currently the most effective survey tool; however, A. planipennis is attracted to some ash volatiles and the color purple. A combination using a large purple-colored sillouhette, baited with an optimal host volatile blend and optimal trap placement, may lead to the development of new survey tools.

INFESTATION DYNAMICS OF THE ASIAN LONGHORNED BEETLE IN THE UNITED STATES

Alan Sawyer

USDA, APHIS, Pest Survey, Detection, and Exclusion Laboratory,
Building 1398, Otis ANGB, MA 02542

ABSTRACT

The Asian longhorned beetle (ALB), *Anoplophora glabripennis* (Coleoptera: Cerambycidae), is an exotic pest of Asian origin, first discovered in North America (Brooklyn, NY) in 1996. That infestation has now spread to Queens, Manhattan and Long Island, NY and Jersey City, NJ. Based on DNA profiles (Carter et al. 2005) and other evidence, independent introductions have occurred in the Chicago area (discovered in 1998), Toronto, Ontario (2003) and Carteret, NJ (2004). The introductions at each site have displayed similar characteristics: a colonization event occurring near an importer of goods from Asia, several years of undetected increase and localized spread, the appearance of satellite infestations at distances ranging from a few hundred meters to 40 km from the point of establishment, and a spatial distribution that is patchy (clumped or aggregated) and self-similar on all spatial scales.

With regard to the ALB, I define "infestation dynamics" to be a sequence of events and component elements comprising (1) introduction from a point of origin in Asia; (2) distribution via shipping to a point of entry in NA; (3) redistribution by air, road, rail or ship from the point of entry to a colonization locale; (4) escape into the environment and initial colonization of one or more host trees; (5) establishment (successful production of a second generation) at the colonization site; (6) within-tree dynamics (increase and spread over time); (7) local dynamics involving natural dispersal to neighboring trees, often of several species; (8) medium-scale dispersal (up to a few km) by flight or with human assistance (in or on vehicles); and (9) large-scale distribution with human assistance (on the order of many km). Infestation dynamics is concerned with population increase or decrease at specific locations, dispersal of individuals, and the changing spatial distribution of the population, resulting in what could be viewed as "behavior" of the infestation, as a whole, in space and time. An infestation exhibits a sequence of characteristics that can be observed, studied, measured and modeled in pursuit of understanding, prediction of future events, and the development of management techniques and strategies.

This paper focuses on within-tree, local and medium-scale dynamics, drawing on data from the U.S. infestations. Techniques have been developed to age egg sites, tunnels and exit holes by examining the tree's growth response to injury. The within-tree dynamics of the ALB has been studied in detail at the Jersey City and Carteret infestations. In Jersey City the locations of all egg sites and the locations and ages of all exit holes were recorded on 102 infested trees. Here the damage was concentrated in the middle and upper portions of infested trees, primarily on or near the bole and major limbs. In contrast, nearly half the damage to 67 infested trees examined in Carteret was found in the lower third of the trees. One red maple in Carteret having over 800 exit holes was dissected carefully, with the locations and ages of all injury sites recorded in each 30 cm section of the entire tree. These data, not yet fully analyzed, will produce a detailed history of population increase and spread within a single tree. The oldest damage on another red maple in Carteret, one having 215 exit holes (66% in the lower third of the tree), dates back to 1998 (> 6 years). Dating all of the exit holes in the lower third (2.4 m) of this tree, it was found that the number of beetles emerging each year were: 1999 (1); 2000 (6); 2001 (14); 2002 (29); 2003 (52); and 2004 (40). The tree, still living but in very bad condition, was removed in December 2004. These data show that the number of beetles emerging approximately doubled each year from 2000 to 2003, but then fell 23 percent in 2004. It appears that following years of exponential increase of the population in the tree, the declining quality or quantity of the resource caused an increase in mortality or emigration from the tree, or both, in 2004. Applying a 2X annual rate of increase to the observed numbers of exit holes in 54 maple trees from Carteret (bearing 1,979 exit holes in all), the numerical and spatial development of the infestation can be inferred. Of the trees examined, the number becoming infested each year and their mean distance from the apparent point of introduction are estimated to have been: 1996: (1 tree, 0 m); 1997: (no trees infested); 1998: (3 trees, 99 m); 1999: (2 trees, 46 m); 2000: (1 tree, 124 m); 2001 (5 trees, 123 m); 2002 (2 trees, 172 m); 2003 (14 trees, 572 m); 2004 (26 trees, 674 m). The exact ages of all of these exit holes must still be determined. The scenario that appears is one of localized population increase and only slow spread for several years, followed by a sudden increase in the number of trees

infested and their distance from the presumed point of first colonization. The data from the Jersey City infestation presents a very similar picture. Data being accumulated from several localized infestations in New York will be analyzed in a similar way. These dispersal distances agree very well with data collected from nearly 1300 infested trees in Chicago, which indicate that the median distance from trees bearing only eggs sites to the nearest tree bearing an older exit hole was less than 20 m, while the 95th and 99th percentiles of the spatial distribution were approximately 125 m and 400 m, respectively.

These results suggest that in areas with abundant host trees, at least, ALB infestations do not spread rapidly. Rather, the population appears to multiply steadily in a limited number of trees for a number of years, then expands suddenly as the condition of the earliest-infested trees deteriorates. If true, this behavior of ALB infestations presents challenges for detecting new introductions, but offers an opportunity to confine and control infestations while they still cover a relatively small area, if detected early. The results gathered to date lend insight into the within-tree distribution of damage and the response of host trees to injury that will help refine survey techniques and permit estimation of probabilities of detection and the date of first infestation. This research has also produced other data on local and medium-scale dynamics that have already helped to define survey, treatment and regulatory strategies.

CLIMATE CHANGE INDUCED INVASIONS BY NATIVE AND EXOTIC PESTS

Jesse A. Logan

USDA Forest Service, Rocky Mountain Research Station, 860 N 1200 E, Logan, UT 84321

The importance of effective risk assessment for introduction and establishment of exotic pest species has dramatically increased with an expanded global economy and the accompanying increase in international trade. Concurrently, recent climate warming has resulted in potential invasion of new habitats by native pest species. The time frame of response to changing climate is much shorter for insects (typically 1 year) than for their host forests (decades or longer). As a result, outbreaks of forest insects, particularly bark beetles, are occurring at unprecedented levels throughout western North America, resulting in the loss of biodiversity and potentially entire ecosystems. In this respect, native species share many characteristics with exotic invasive species. Due to the rapidly changing ecological landscape resulting from climate warming, the historic paradigm by which we view "native species," "exotic species," and "invasive species" is in need of revision. The primary goal of this presentation is to articulate an expanded and more flexible paradigm that relates these three important concepts.

An expanded contextual framework that includes the concept of a "native-invasive species" is shown in Fig. 1.

Mountain pine beetle outbreak in the Sawtooth National Recreation Area. The Sawtooth National Recreational Area (SNRA) in central Idaho is one of the most scenic regions in the western United States. This area has also been the site for long-term research on mountain pine

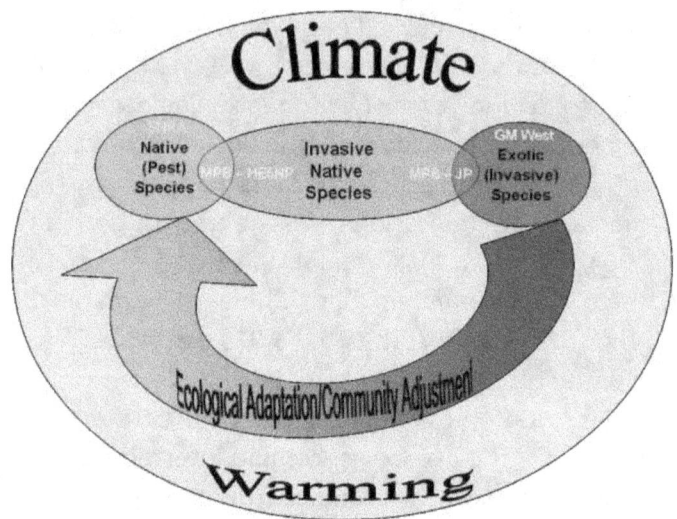

Figure 1. The historically exclusive concepts of native and exotic species are still valid; however, the rapid environmental change resulting from factors like climate warming are blurring the boundaries between these traditional categories. Changing climate has allowed some opportunistic species to invade new, heretofore-inaccessible, habitats. The interconnected relationship shown will be illustrated by four examples.

beetle population dynamics for the USDA Forest Service Western Bark Beetle Project. The reason for this long-term commitment is not because the SNRA is a nice place to work (although it is!) rather it results from the meso-environment provided by the Stanley Basin in the heart of the SNRA. This basin, which is home to the headwaters of the Salmon River, has historically been too cold for outbreak populations to develop. This attribute allowed detailed life-history studies to be conducted in the same geographical area for a prolonged period of time (beginning in the late 1980s). Researchers simply followed small spot infestations from one thermally favorable microhabitat (typically on the west-facing, east side of the valley) to another, year after year. However, beginning in the mid 1990s something very different began to happen. The individual spot infestations began to merge into building outbreak populations. The final result was a full-scale, exponentially expanding, outbreak over the years 1995-2003. Concurrent with this outbreak were model simulations that predicted a shift from asynchronous, fractional voltinism to synchronous univoltinism (Powell and Logan 2005). Beginning in 1995, and every year after, model predictions have been for an adaptive seasonality that is basic to outbreak development. Although unusual in that a full-blown outbreak occurred in an area thought to be climatically unsuitable, it is still an example of a native species operating in a co-evolved (lodgepole pine forest) habitat resilient to mountain pine beetle outbreak disturbances.

Mountain pine beetle in high-elevation five-needle pine ecosystems. Viewing a landscape like the SNRA through the "eyes" of the mountain pine beetle results in an altitudinal partitioning of the landscape. In this regard, the SNRA is typical of many mountain valleys in the middle Rocky Mountains. The extreme elevational gradient, and subsequent orographic effect on climate, results in adaptive seasonality in the lodgepole pine forests along the valley margins, fractional voltinism at intermediate elevations typically occupied by nonhost spruce-fir forests, and synchronous semivoltine populations (maladaptive climate) in the high-elevation pine forests (Logan and Bentz 1999). Whitebark pine is an example of a high-elevation forest that has historically been climatically unsuited for outbreak populations of the mountain pine beetle (Logan & Powell 2001). Of the high-elevation pines, whitebark pine is of particular ecological importance, and serves as a keystone or foundation species for these sensitive ecosystems (Lanner 1996).

Although historically whitebark pine habitats have been too severe for outbreak populations of mountain pine beetles, a widespread outbreak occurred in this forest type during the1930s. Motivated by this unusual event, and also because computer simulations indicated a potential shift in suitability of high-elevation systems with reasonable global warming scenarios (Logan and Bentz 1999), we established a long-term study site in whitebark pine at Railroad Ridge (elevation 10,000 ft) in the White Cloud Mountains of central Idaho. Although model predictions indicated an adaptive seasonality by mid-century, outbreak populations began to be expressed in 2003, and a full-scale epidemic is now under way. In many respects (warming resulting in adaptive seasonality expressed as a threshold event that would abruptly become much more favorable for the mountain pine beetle) our model predictions were accurate, with the exception that outbreaks occurred much earlier than expected. The reason for this surprise relates directly to the nature of climate change (expressed more intensely at high elevations and latitudes than the global average) and to the ecology of mountain pine beetle operating as an invasive species in an ecosystem apparently not co-evolved with epidemic bark beetle disturbance.

Recently (summers 2003, 2004), it has become apparent that dramatic changes are occurring across a wide geographic range of whitebark pine. Motivated by these changes we have performed model simulations predicting impacts in sensitive regions such as the Greater Yellowstone Area. Example simulations are provided in Fig. 2.

Comparing simulation results in Fig. 2 indicates that the significant impacts of mountain pine beetle outbreaks will intensify as climate continues to warm. Simulations also indicate that some areas (e.g. the Wind River Mountains) are not projected to see increased risk from mountain pine beetle outbreaks. These areas may provide key refugia for this keystone species, and strategic

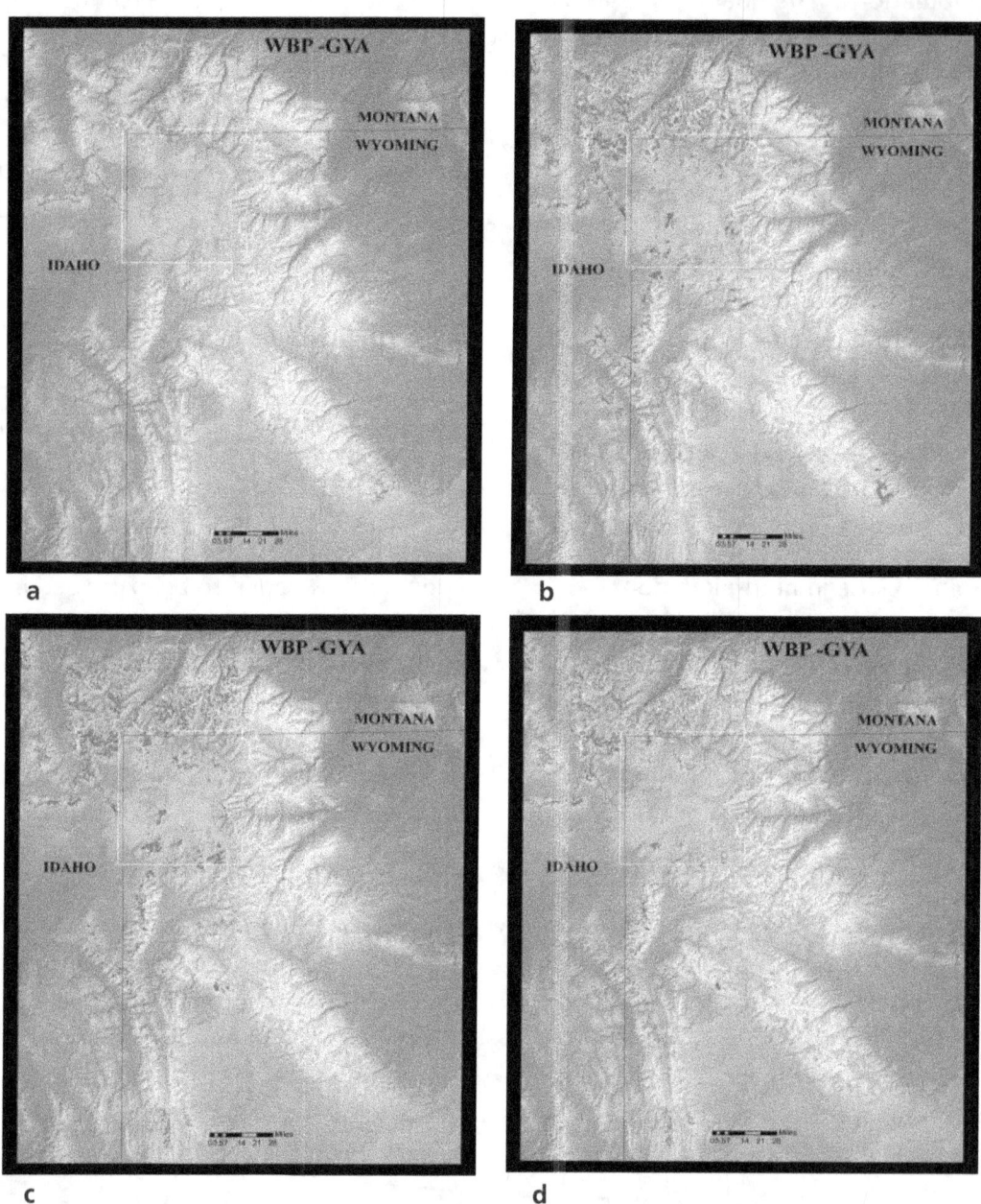

Figure 2. Simulations of mountain pine beetle adaptive seasonality for the greater Yellowstone area. Yellowstone National Park is outlined in white. Red indicates whitebark pine with probability of adaptive seasonality ≥ 0.5. a: Pre-warming climate based on temperature normals for 1951-1980. b: Current climate base on 1981-2010 normals [historic and VEMAP (Kittel et al. 1995) projected climate]. c: Projected warming (VEMAP) based on 2031-2060 normals. d: Historic normals (1921-1950) centered on the 1930s.

conservation efforts should be directed to these areas provided that the historical simulations prove to be accurate (i.e. ground surveys confirm that these areas did not sustain significant mortality during the 1930s).

Considering the invasive species paradigm of Fig. 1, although low-level or endemic populations of mountain pine beetles have probably always existed in whitebark pine ecosystems, it is clear that the nature of this interaction has dramatically changed. This characteristic is basic to the description of an invasive-native species. The bottom line is: as long as climate warming continues, whitebark pine as a species and ecosystem is at high risk for loss over much of its geographic distribution.

Mountain pine beetle range expansion and potential invasion of the boreal forest. Historically, the northern limits to mountain pine beetle distribution have been climatically determined. Host lodgepole pine forests extend much further north than do mountain pine beetles. The distribution to the east has been limited by the previously insurmountable barriers of the Great Plains in the United States, and the continental divide in Canada. However, simulations with CO_2 doubling climate change scenarios (Logan and Powell 2001) indicated the potential for significant range expansion to the north. The distributions of lodgepole pine and jack pine significantly overlap, with a hybrid zone that is within the predicted range expansion. These model predictions were particularly germane because the largest mountain pine beetle outbreak ever recorded was under way in British Columbia (10 million ha affected by summer 2005).

The ongoing mountain pine beetle outbreak in Canada is not only unprecedented in size but also in location, far north of previously observed outbreaks (Carroll et al. 2004). During the summer of 2003, large numbers of dispersing mountain pine beetles were apparently caught by westerly winds associated with a major frontal storm system. These beetles were transported across the continental divide at the furthest north and lowest of the six major passes through the Canadian Cordillera, appropriately named Pine Pass (less than 1000 m in elevation). Transported beetles from this, and perhaps other similar events, have resulted in established populations where they have not previously existed—on the east side of the continental divide, ranging south almost to Jasper, B.C. Spot infestations are now within 50 km of the boreal jack pine forest (A. Carroll, personal communication). If invasive populations of mountain pine beetles become established in jack pine, there is contiguous host pine forest across the continent all the way to the loblolly forests of the southeastern United States (Logan and Powell 2004). We may be on the verge of a biogeographical event of continental scale with devastating economic and ecological consequences.

Enhanced establishment risk for an exotic invasive species. Gypsy moth is a serious defoliating insect that was introduced into Massachusetts in the mid 1880s. Since that time, it has expanded its range throughout the deciduous forest of the northeast and central United Sates, and southeastern Canada. Given the influx of immigrants and tourists from infested areas into the Interior West, multiple gypsy moth introductions are made, and many are detected, every year. This region also has extensive susceptible landscapes comprised of several species favored by gypsy moth; namely aspen, oaks and various maples. In spite of abundant potential host species, these introductions have yet to result in established populations. The success of eradication efforts, and the unsuccessful establishment of many detected and undetected introductions, likely result from an inhospitable climate. Climatic suitability for gypsy moth in the western United States, however, is potentially improving, perhaps rapidly, due to a general warming trend that began in the mid 1970s and continues today.

Motivated by the challenge of assessing the risk for establishment of detected introductions, a research/technology transfer project was funded by U.S. Forest Service, Forest Health Protection, to implement a gypsy moth risk assessment program for the interior western United States, with Utah as the example state. This system, GMWest, interfaces weather and climate with a gypsy moth adaptive seasonality model to project risk of establishment across the landscape of interest (Logan et al. submitted). This integrated system was then used to evaluate climate change scenarios for native host species in Utah, with the result that risk of establishment will dramatically increase during the remainder of the 21st century under conservative climate change scenarios. Figure 3 compares current with predicted end-century risk probability for gypsy moth establishment.

GMWest was then applied for risk assessment of several case histories of detected gypsy moth introductions in Utah. These applications demonstrated the general utility of the system for predicting risk of establishment and for designing improved risk detection.

Summary–The expanded flexibility required for an inclusive paradigm for native, exotic and invasive species provided in Fig. 1 was illustrated by four examples. These examples can be summarized as:

SNRA mountain pine beetle outbreak in lodgepole pine, and within the historic distribution of mountain pine beetle in Canada:

- Although the attributes of outbreaks may be altered, these changes are occurring within a system that is ecologically resilient (co-adapted) to mountain pine beetle disturbances. This example, therefore, fits the classic definition of a native pest species outbreak.

Mountain pine beetle in whitebark pine:

- This is an example of a basic shift in the ecological role of mountain pine beetle from a fugitive saprophyte to an aggressive predator.

- Mountain pine beetle outbreak dynamics are unusually explosive in these systems.

- For various reasons, high elevation pine ecosystems are particularly vulnerable to mountain pine beetle disturbances.

- There is the potential for loss of whitebark pine over much of its distribution through the combined action of an introduce pathogen (white pine blister rust) acting in consort with mountain pine beetle outbreaks.

- This example is clearly different from a classic outbreak of a native pest species, and embodies many of the concerns historically associated with an exotic-invasive species, i.e., it is acting as a native-invasive species, even though historically it has been present in the ecosystem.

Mountain pine beetle invasion potential for jack pine forests:

- If mountain pine beetle successfully colonizes jack pine, it will clearly be a native-invasive pest in a novel ecosystem.

- Economic consequences are obvious and immediate.

- Ecological consequences are speculative but potentially devastating due to the interconnectedness of the boreal forest with eastern North America pines.

Enhanced probability of gypsy moth establishment in the western United States:

- This is a classic example of an exotic-invasive species.

- Risk assessment for establishment of introduced gypsy moths is complicated by the effects of climate warming.

- Effective technologies (computer models, GIS) exist that dramatically assist the risk assessment process.

Finally, gypsy moth in the eastern United States was mentioned as an example that fits the role of an exotic introduction species in a transitional state of assimilation into native ecosystems.

Literature Cited

Carroll, A., S. Taylor, J. Regniere, and L. Safranyik. 2004. **Effects of climate change on range expansion by the mountain pine** beetle **in British Columbia**. pp. 223-232, In T.L. Shore, J.E. Brooks, and J.E. Stone, (eds.) **Mountain Pine Beetle Symposium: Challenges and Solutions, October 30-31, 2003, Kelowna, British Columbia, Canada. Natural Resources Canada, Canadian Forest Service, Pacific Forestry Centre, Victoria, British Columbia,** Information Report BC-X-399.

Kittel, T.G.F., N. A. Rosenbloom, T. H. Painter, and D. S. Schimel. 1995. The VEMAP **integrated database for modeling United States ecosystem/vegetation sensitive to climate change**. J. Biogeography 22: 857-862.

Lanner, R. M. 1996. **Made for each other: a symbiosis of birds and pines**. Oxford University Press, New York.

Logan, J. A., and B. J. Bentz. 1999. **Model analysis of mountain pine beetle seasonality**. Environ. Entomol. 28: 924-934.

Logan, J. A., and J. A. Powell. 2001. **Ghost forests, global warming, and the mountain pine beetle**. Am. Entomol. 47: 160-173.

Logan, J. A., and J. A. Powell. 2004. **Modelling mountain pine beetle phenological response to temperature**. pp. 210-222, In T.L. Shore, J.E. Brooks, and J.E. Stone (eds.), Mountain Pine Beetle Symposium: Challenges and Solutions, October 30-31, 2003, Kelowna, British Columbia, Canada. Natural Resources Canada, Canadian Forest Service, Pacific Forestry Centre, Victoria, British Columbia, Information Report BC-X-399.

Logan, J. A., J. Régnière, D. R. Gray, and A. S. Munson. 2007. **Risk assessment in face of a changing environment: gypsy moth and climate change in Utah**. Ecol. Appl. (in press).

Powell, J. A., and J. A. Logan. 2005. **Insect seasonality: circle map analysis of temperature-driven life cycles**. Theor. Popul. Biol. 67: 161-179.

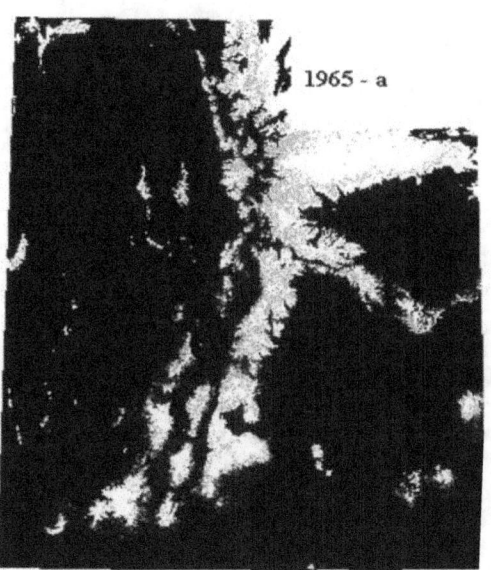
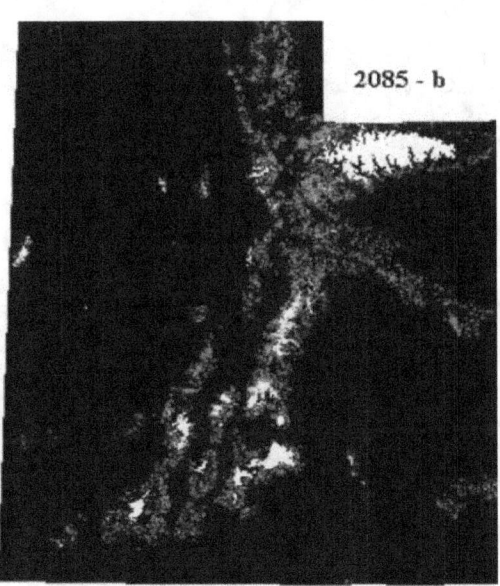

Figure 3. Black area indicates adaptive climate (P ≥ 0.5) for gypsy moth establishment. White area indicates climate is not adaptive (P ≤ 0.5) for gypsy moth establishment. Green indicates aspen in white area, red is aspen in the black area. Under current climatic conditions, approximately 10 percent of the aspen in the state was at high risk for establishment, and most of this was at the fringe of the aspen distribution. By end of the century more than 90 percent of aspen is projected to be at high risk.

NATIONAL INVASIVE SPECIES PROGRAM

Anna Rinick and Hilda Diaz-Soltero

United States Department of Agriculture, Washington, DC

ABSTRACT

The structure and function of the National Invasive Species Council was presented below. The names and contact information for the USDA Invasive Species coordinators as of February 2006 were presented on the next page.

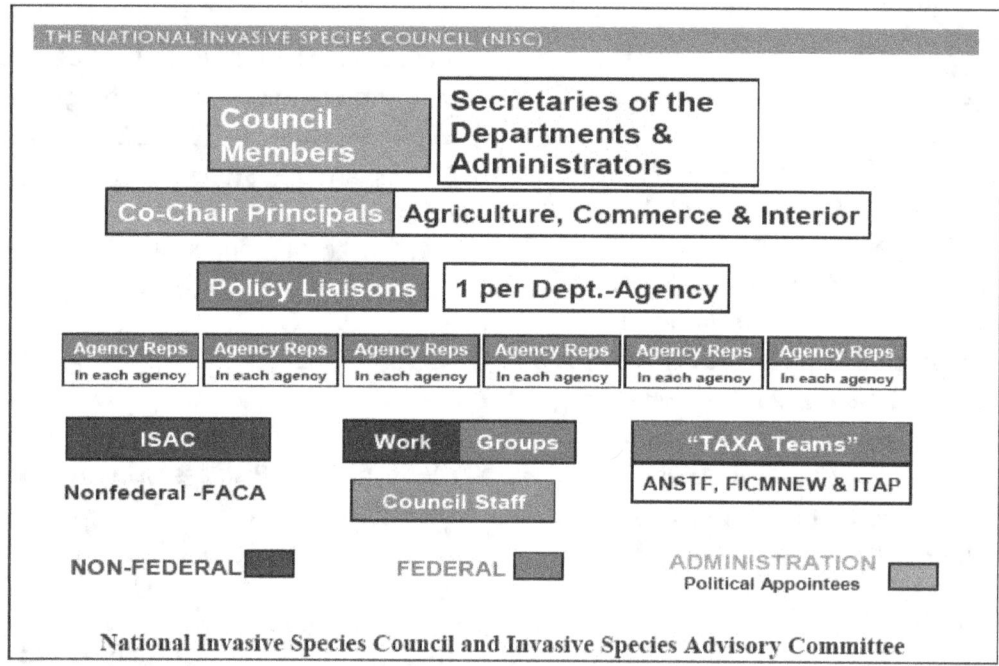

National Invasive Species Council and Invasive Species Advisory Committee

NISC / ISAC FACA-Chartered Task Teams/Subcommittees

1) Leadership and Coordination
2) Communications, Education and Outreach
3) Control, Management and Restoration
4) Early Detection and Rapid Response
5) Information Management
6) International Cooperation
7) Research
8) Definitions
9) Prevention (Joint with ANSTF)
    1) Pathways
    2) Screening
    3) Risk Analysis

GENERAL OBSERVATIONS:

1. To date, NISC staff has had some contact with more than **2000** individuals that are engaged on the issue.

2. About **300** federal/state/private programs, **140** groups & **170** organizations have at least some involvement with invasive species.

3. Approximately **35** federal agencies and **24** federal laws have some role/impact in invasive species.

TAXA TEAMS--FICMNEW: *Federal Interagency Committee for the Management of Noxious and Exotic Weeds; ANSTF: Aquatic Nuisance Species Taskforce; ITAP: Invasive Terrestrial Animals and Pathogens Team.*

USDA Invasive Species Coordinators February, 2006

Name	Agency	E-Mail	Telephone/FAX Number
Hilda Diaz-Soltero**	USDA	hdiazsoltero@fs.fed.us	202-354-1880/ 371-1751
James Tuck	APHIS	james.m.tuck@aphis.usda.gov	301-734-5819/734-6357
Kevin Hackett	ARS	kjh@ars.usda.gov	301-504-4680/ 504-6191
Ernest S. Delfosse	ARS	esd@ars.usda.gov	301-504-6470/ 504-6191
Rick Bennett	ARS	rbrnnett@ars.usda.gov	301-504-6915/ 504-6490
Bob Nowierski	CSREES	rnowierski@csrees.usda.gov	202-401-4900/ 401-4888
Herb Bolton	CSREES	hbolton@csrees.usda.gov	202-401-4201/ 401-4888
Utpal Vasavada	ERS	vasavada@ers.usda.gov	202-694-5540/ 694-5575
Mary Bohman	ERS	mbohman@ers.usda.gov	202-694-5500/ 694-5792
Janet Perry	ERS	jperry@ers.usda.gov	202-694-5152/ 694-
Larry Bryant	FS	lbryant01@fs.fed.us	202-205-0850/ 205-1096
Bob Lange	FS	boblange@fs.fed.us	202-205-2773 / 205-1096
Michael Ielmini	FS/NFS	mielmini@fs.fed.us	202-205-1049/ 205-1096
Gary Smith	FS/S&PF	gsmith03@fs.fed.us	704-605-5342/703-605-5353
Mary Ellen Dix	FS/R&D	mdix@fs.fed.us	703-605-5260/ 605-5133
Doug Holy	NRCS	doug.holy@wdc.usda.gov	202-720-9096/ 720-2646
Scott Peterson	NRCS	scott.peterson@la.usda.gov	225-775-6280/
Robert Escheman	NRCS	Robert.Escheman@wdc.usda.gov	202-720-0536/ 720-2646
Jamie.Green	OBPA	jfg@obpa.usda.gov	202-720-2881
Paula Geiger	OBPA	pal@obpa.usda.gov	202-720-2385/ 720-8635
Mark Smith	OBPA	mes@obpa.usda.gov	202-720-4509/ 720-3258

**Senior USDA Invasive Species Coordinator

Glossary of abbreviations:

APHIS – Animal and Plant Health Inspection Service
ARS – Agricultural Research Service
CSREES – Cooperative State Research, Education and Extension Service
ERS – Economic Research Service
USFS – U.S. Forest Service
FSA – Farm Service Agency
ISAC – Invasive Species Advisory Committee
NISC – National Invasive Species Council
NRCS – Natural Resources Conservation Service
OBPA – Office of Budget and Program Analysis
USDA – United States Department of Agriculture

HOST RANGE OF THE EMERALD ASH BORER (*AGRILUS PLANIPENNIS*) (COLEOPTERA: BURPRESTIDAE): CHOICE AND NO-CHOICE TESTS

Andrea C. Anulewicz[1], Deborah G. McCullough[1,2], David A. Cappaert[2], Therese R. Poland[3] and Deborah L. Miller[3]

[1]Department of Forestry, Michigan State University, 243 Natural Science Building, East Lansing, MI 48824
[2]Department of Entomology, Michigan State University, 243 Natural Science Building, East Lansing, MI 48824
[3]USDA Forest Service, North Central Research Station, 1407 South Harrison Rd., Ste. 220, East Lansing, MI 48824

ABSTRACT

Previous literature on the emerald ash borer (EAB) suggests that, in its native range in Asia, EAB will attack species other than ash (*Fraxinus*), including *Ulmus* sp. and *Juglans* sp. In North America, as ash trees die in the core zone of infestation, concern has been raised about the potential for species other than ash to act as a suitable host for this pest. If an alternate host species were to be discovered, the impact on forest resources would increase dramatically in North America.

Our objectives were to 1) determine if EAB can oviposit and develop on potential alternate host species; and 2) evaluate preference among four North American species of ash. We evaluated early instar development on logs of ash and potential alternate hosts that were placed in infested ash trees and in choice and no-choice tests using live nursery trees. We studied four ash species common in Michigan: green ash (*F. pennsylvanica*), white ash (*F. americana*), black ash (*F. nigra*), and blue ash (*F. quadrangulata*). Potential alternate host species included American elm (*U. americana*), black walnut (*J. nigra*), and Japanese tree lilac (*Syringa reticulate*).

In 2004, 40 nursery trees including 10 green ash, 10 white ash, 10 Japanese tree lilac, and 10 black walnut, were transplanted in Ann Arbor, MI. Male and female beetles were caged on the lower 1 m section of the stem of each tree throughout the summer. The uncaged portions of the trees were exposed to wild beetle populations for the duration of the natural flight season. All trees were harvested and dissected during the winter.

In 2004, there were approximately 35 galleries/m² on the caged green ash stems, 0.8 galleries/m² on the caged white ash stems, and no galleries on tree lilac or walnut. On the upper, uncaged sections of the trees, we recorded approx. 150 and 75 galleries/m² on green and white ash trees, respectively. No galleries were found on tree lilac or walnut. More than 65 percent of the galleries on green ash trees were on trees with rough bark.

In 2003, logs of green ash, walnut, and elm were attached to the main stem of infested green ash trees, 5 to 7 meters above the ground. In 2004, white ash and blue ash logs were added to the study and logs were attached to infested white ash trees. For both studies, less than four galleries were found on walnut and none were found on elm. Nearly 200 galleries per m² were found on green ash in 2003 and on white ash in 2004. This study was repeated in 2005 at two sites with predominately green ash trees and two sites with predominately white ash trees. One green and one white ash log were placed in each tree along with a third log that was either black or blue ash or black walnut. At three of the four sites, the green ash logs had higher gallery densities than the other ash species. At one site, gallery density on white ash logs was greater than the other ash species. Approximately 150 abnormal, unsuccessful, feeding attempts were made on seven of the twelve black walnut logs.

Overall, our results to date show that EAB females will land and oviposit on species other than ash. However, early instar feeding is limited and development is substantially impaired in non-ash species in both lab and field studies.

BUD GALL MIDGES – POTENTIAL INVADERS
ON LARCHES IN NORTH AMERICA

Yuri N. Baranchikov

[1]V.N. Sukachev Institute of Forest, Siberian Branch, Russian Academy of Science
50 Akademgorodok, Krasnoyarsk 660039

ABSTRACT

Larch bud gall midges (Diptera: Cecidomyiidae) form a specialized group of gall insects inhabiting buds of larch (*Larix*) in the northern Palaearctic Region. Currently there are four described species in this group. *Dasineura kellneri* Henschel is found in Central Europe and infests *Larix decidua*; *D. rozhkovi* Mam.et Nik. is widely distributed through southern and eastern Siberia to Khabarovsk and in northeastern Mongolia on *L. sibirica*, *L. gmelinii*, and *L. czekanowskii*; *D. verae* Skuhrava is known from Southern Siberia and Northern Mongolia on *L. sibirica*, *L. gmelinii* ; *D. nipponica* Inouye was described from Japan and lives on *L. kaempferi*.

Species of midges differ both in morphology of adults and in gall structure. In general, all midges modify larch buds into an artichoke-like galls in the center if needle clusters. Gall-bearing buds die. During persistent and heavy infestations trees may lose up to 90 percent of their buds. Such trees produce no flower buds, so commercial seed production is impossible. Nowadays, the midge *D. rozhkovi* is the primary biological factor affecting productivity of larch seed orchards in Russia. Even though badly infested, trees do not die because new twigs are formed annually on gall-bearing branches.

All larch gall midges are highly specialized herbivores with a 1-year life cycle. The flight period of adult midges is synchronized with the initiation of larch needle growth in early spring and the flight period is very short: 3-4 days with nearly 60 percent of adults hatching in one day. Fecundity is rather constant, at 60-85 eggs per female.

Females oviposit between the needles and bract scales of spur shoots. Larvae hatch in 6-9 days and crawl between the needles to the vegetative cone of the next year's bud, which is situated in the center of the needle cluster. Substances secreted by the larvae modify the buds' morphogenesis: the folia primordia start growing and produce scales instead of needles. The galls become visible in early June and stop growth in 1-2 months. The base of the galled bud increases and the scales closing it, form a larval chamber, in which the insect develops.

Larvae feed at the bud apex by sucking food substances from plant tissues. In August the fourth instar larvae weave a thick white cocoon for overwintering. *D. kellnery* and *D. nipponica* make a cocoon in the larval chamber; *D. rozhkovi* leaves the chamber and overwinters between external gall scales; finally, larvae of *D. verae* leave the tree and overwinter in forest litter. Larvae of all species pupate the following spring in the cocoon; in 5-7 days the new adults emerge.

The adaptive potential of the most damaging species—*D. rozhkovi*—was studied at the graft plantation of larches in Krasnoyarsk Kray. In fewer than 17 generations the gall midge population inhabiting *L. sibirica* in the vicinity, colonized the crowns of *L. gmelinii*, *L. ochotensis*, *L. sukachevii*, *L. decidua* and (important!) *L. laricina*. All larch species differ in time of bud burst and in a short period of time the dynamics of adult midge emergence in gall insect demes was observed to differ between host trees species according to their phenology.

Currently there are no insect herbivores inhabiting the buds of larches in Northern America. Random introductions of Palaearctic species of gall midges, especially the most aggressive *D. rozhkovi* could quickly occupy this empty ecological space.

THE RUSSIANS ARE COMING–AREN'T THEY?
SIBERIAN MOTH IN EUROPEAN FORESTS

Yuri N. Baranchikov[1], Vladimir M. Pet'ko[1] and Vladimir L. Ponomarev[2]

[1]V.N. Sukachev Institute of Forest, Siberian Branch, Russian Academy of Science
50 Akademgorodok, Krasnoyarsk 660039

[2]Institute of Chemical Means for Plant Protection,
31 Ugreshskaya Str., Moscow 115088

ABSTRACT

Dendrolimus superans sibiricus Tschtv. (Lepidoptera: Lasiocampidae) is the most destructive defoliator of the coniferous taiga forest in Siberia and the Russian Far East. Outbreaks of this pest species are the primary biological factor influencing change in forest cover in the southern taiga subzone with enormous ecological and social consequences (Baranchikov et al. 2001). The species has a range that extends from the Pacific Ocean (Russian Far East, Japan and Northern Korea) across Siberia, Northern China and Mongolia to the Ural Mountains (Rozhkov 1963). At the beginning of the 20th century the species was documented to have spread 500 km to the west of the Urals to the Republic of Udmurtiya.

Since the year 2000, a 1:1 mixture of aldehyde Z,E-5,7-dodecadienal and alcohol Z,E-5,7-dodecadienol has been used in pheromone traps to monitor Siberian moth populations in the Asian part of Russia (Baranchikov et al. 2000, Klun et al. 2000, Pletnev et al. 2000). In 2001, a series of traps were placed in the center of European Russia. Many males were caught in the Republic of Mariy El (500 km east of Moscow); two moths were even trapped in a Moscow neighborhood (Lebedeva et al. 2005). Unfortunately the absence of insecticide strips in the traps did not protect the captured specimens and all were damaged making an accurate identification difficult. The trapped moths were automatically referred to *D.s.sibiricus*. These results received enormous international attention (Gninenko & Orlinskii 2002). The Panel on Quarantine Pests for Forestry of European and Mediterranean Plant Protection Organization (EPPO) added Siberian moth to the EPPO A2 quarantine list as a species of serious risk for the forests of Byelorussia, Poland, Baltic and Scandinavian countries. This action automatically demands special plant health certificates on all imports of Russian raw timber and it may have serious economic consequences (EPPO 2005). For example, Finland imports 6 million m^3 of Russian timber every year in about 150,000 shipments. If every shipment has to have its own pest-free certificate, the inevitable delays and confusion at the borders could shut down the sawmills and pulp mills of Eastern Finland and will slow wood exports from Russia.

In June-July 2004, we tested different mixtures of Z,E-5,7-dodecadienal and Z,E-5,7-dodecadienol in the Scots pine forests in the foothills of the eastern Sayan mountains in the southern part of Krasnoyarsk Kray—the mutual habitat of two species of *Dendrolimus*: *D. superans* and *D. pini* (pine moth). Pine moth is a common pest of pine in the western Palaearctic Region. It is distributed from Western and Northern Europe through southern Siberia to Transbaikalia. We used box carton traps with insecticide strips and folgaplen dispensers (Baranchikov 2003).

Both the pheromone and the dispensers were manufactured by the Institute of Chemical Means for Plant Protection in Moscow. Five different mixtures of attractant (Table 1) were tested in 10 replicates. The traps were placed in a line 150 m apart in 1-2-3-4-5-1-2 etc. sequence in a park type pine forest. For a period of 40 days traps were checked twice—23 males of *D. pini* and 17 males of *D. superans* were caught. The distribution of catches demonstrated that 1:1 and 1:0.5 mixtures had equal attractivity to both species. The 1:0.1 mixture was not attractive for Siberian moth males and the aldehyde did not attract either species.

The experiment demonstrated the similarity of sex attractants of Siberian moth and pine moth. Possibly the pheromones of these species, in addition to the main components, contain some minor ones which determine the specificity of the communication signal. Males of the two species are morphologically very similar, the only real difference can be found in male genitalia. The lower branch of the valvae of Siberian moth is much longer and thinner than that of the pine moth (Fig. 1).

Table 1. Attractivity of different mixtures and concentrations of Z,E-5,7-dodecadienal (Z5E7DDDAL) and Z,E-5,7-dodecadienol (Z5E7DDDOL) for males of two Dendrolimus species in Krasnoyarsk Kray

Attractant components mkg per lure Z5E7DDDAL:Z5E7DDDOL	% of the total males caught	
	Dendrolimus pini	*D. superans sibiricus*
1 1000 : 1000	30.4	41.2
2 1000 : 500	39.1	47.1
3 1000 : 250	8.7	11.7
4 1000 : 100	21.8	0.0
5 1000 : 0	0.0	0.0
Total	100	100

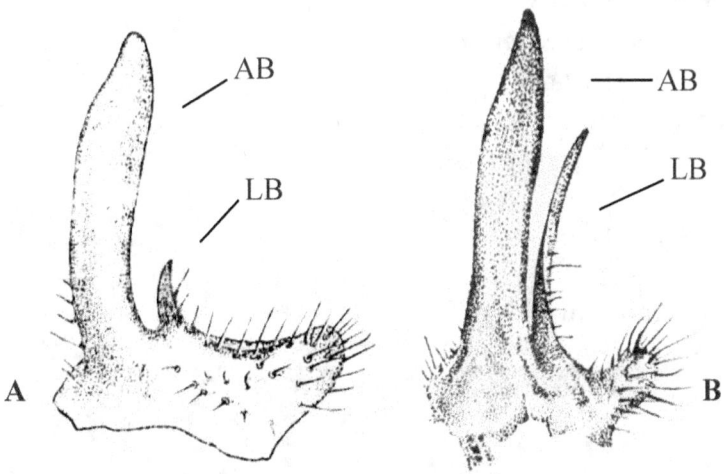

Figure 1. Part of genitalia (valvae) of Dendrolimus pini (A) and D. superans sibiricus (B) males; AB – upper branch, LB—lower branch of valvae.

In the regions occupied by both species of *Dendrolimus* use of Siberian moth sex attractant in pheromone traps should be accompanied by an obligatory morphological examination of male genitalia. During the summer 2004, the 500:500 mkg per lure mixture of aldehyde and alcohol attracted *Dendrolimus* males in a few areas of Lithuania (Ponomarev et al. 2005). The morphological analysis of samples proved it was *D. pini*, not Siberian moth. Morphology of moths trapped in Mariy El and near Moscow in 2001 was not studied.

To conclude, for the moment there is no definitive evidence of Siberian moth occurring in the center of the European part of Russia. Both the structure and species composition of European forests are quite unfavorable for this pest. Its complex life cycle with obligate winter and facultative summer diapause of larvae strongly depends on photoperiod and temperature and will complicate the process of local adaptation. The possibility of Siberian moth distribution to Western and Northern Europe is highly questionable.

Literature Cited

Baranchikov Yu.N., Kondakov Yu.P., Petrenko E.S. 2001. **Catastrophic outbreaks of Siberian moth in Krasnoyarsk Kray.** *In*: National Security of Russia. Krasnoyarsk Kray. Znaniye: Moscow: 146-167 (in Russian).

Baranchikov Yu.N., Petko V.M. 2003. **Attraction of Siberian moth males by different dispensers and pheromone concentrations.** Proceedings, USDA Interagency Research Forum on Gypsy Moth and Other Invasive Species, GTR-NE-315: 8.

EPPO, 2005. **Data sheets on quarantine pests:** *Dendrolimus sibiricus* and *Dendrolimus* [sic] **superans.** Web version 2005-09. European and Mediterranean Plant Protection Organization. (http://www.eppo.org/QUARANTINE/insects/*Dendrolimus sibiricus*/DSDENDSI.pdf).

Gninenko Yu.I., Orlinskii A.D. 2002. ***Dendrolimus sibiricus* in the coniferous forests of European Russia at the beginning of the twenty-first century.** EPPO Bulletin, 332: 481-483.

Lebedeva K.V., Vendilo N.V., Pletnev V.A., Mitroshin D.B., Gninenko Yu.I. 2005. **Pheromone preparation "Denalol" for forest protection from the Siberian moth.** Lesnoye Khozyaistvo, 2: 44-46 (in Russian).

Ponomarev V.L., Baranchikov Yu.N., Pet'ko V.M., Marchenko Ya.I., Ostrauskas G.G. 2005. **Field testing of *Dendrolimus pini* L. sex pheromone.** Lesnoy Vestnik, Moscow, 35: 145-151 (in Russian).

Rozhkov A.S. 1963. **Siberian moth.** USSR Academy of Science, Moscow, 176 p. (in Russian).

NEMATODES FOR THE BIOLOGICAL CONTROL OF THE WOODWASP, *SIREX NOCTILIO*

Robin A. Bedding

CSIRO Entomology, PO Box 1700, ACT 2601, Australia

ABSTRACT

The tylenchid nematode *Beddingia* (*Deladenus*) *siricidicola* (Bedding) is by far the most important control agent of Sirex noctilio F., a major pest of pine plantations. It sterilizes female sirex, is density dependent, can achieve nearly 100 percent parasitism and, as a result of its complicated biology can be readily manipulated for sirex control. Bedding and Iede (2005) gave a comprehensive account of this nematode and its use in Australia and South America.

Throughout the 1960s and early 1970s, CSIRO and various consultants conducted a comprehensive search, in hundreds of localities from Europe, USA, Canada, India, Pakistan, Turkey, Morocco and Japan, for coniferous trees infested with any siricid species. Thousands of logs from these trees were then caged in quarantine, mainly at Silwood Park, UK, where all emerging insects were investigated for biological control potential. As a result of these collections, seven species of *Beddingia* were found parasitising 19 siricids (associated with two fungal symbionts) and 12 parasitoids from 31 tree species and 29 countries (Bedding and Akhurst 1978). Only one species of nematode, *B. siricidicola*, was found to be suitable for sirex control and this has now been released and established in Australia, New Zealand, Brazil, Uruguay, Argentina and South Africa.

B. siricidicola is extraordinary in having two separate life cycles associated with two morphologically very different adult female types (Bedding 1967, 1968, 1972). In the parasitic cycle, 5 to 20 mm long, cylindrical, often green-colored females release thousands of juvenile nematodes into the body cavity of adult sirex wasps. In the free-living cycle 1 to 2 mm long females feed on the symbiotic fungus, *Amylostereum areolatum* (Fr.) Boidin as it grows in the tree, and lay eggs in the tracheids (wood fibers). (These two types of females are so morphologically different from each other that each on its own would have been placed in a separate family of nematodes. Poinar et al. [2002] have now placed both forms of *Beddingia* species in a new family, the Beddingiidae).

At about the time adult parasitized sirex emerge from infested trees, adult nematodes have usually released most of the juveniles that are within them into the insect's blood cavity and the juveniles have migrated to the insect's reproductive organs. In the male, this is a dead end but female sirex are effectively sterilized because, as well as ovarial development being suppressed to various degrees, each egg that is produced is filled with up to 200 juvenile nematodes. A parasitized female sirex still oviposits readily, and often in several different trees, but lays packets of nematodes instead of viable eggs. Since many sirex often attack the same trees, larval progeny of unparasitised sirex can eventually become infected with nematodes, but this is only made likely by the many intervening free-living cycles which enable the nematode to breed through the tree in vast numbers. It is only when juvenile nematodes reach the immediate microenvironment around sirex larvae that they are stimulated by high CO_2 and low pH (Bedding 1993) to develop into the preparasitic kind of female rather than the fungal-feeding form. After mating the infective female uses its large anterior spear-like stylet to bore into sirex larvae and within a few weeks of penetrating a larva the nematode grows up to 1000-fold in volume. It now remains, often for several months, relatively unchanged, until the sirex larva pupates. Then the nematode's reproductive system develops rapidly from a few cells to produce many thousands of juvenile nematodes in little more than a week, and these are released into the insect's blood cavity at about the time the insect emerges from the tree.

The fungal-feeding life cycle is not only important in enabling high levels of parasitism in sirex populations, it can be used to manipulate the nematode for biological control purposes. Initially it was possible to maintain a library of hundreds of isolates of the various nematode species and strains on fungi growing on agar slopes which were kept under refrigeration for many years while being evaluated as control agents. In addition, once the best species/strain had been selected, it could be sterilely mass reared, for liberation, in flasks of autoclaved wheat/rice inoculated with *A. areolatum*.

Selecting the best nematode species for liberation from the library of stored isolates was relatively simple; only two species fed on *A. areolatum* (the symbiont of *S. noctilio*) and one of these *B. wilsoni* was excluded because it parasitised rhysinne parasitoids. However, there still remained hundreds of isolates of *B. siricidicola* from 20 countries, 10 tree species and four sirex species. The best strain, from Sopron in Hungary, was selected because it totally sterilizes female *S. noctilio*, gives the highest levels of parasitism and unlike strains that fulfilled the first two criteria, has little effect on the size of sirex emerging from logs correctly inoculated with it. (The large size of parasitized sirex is important because they fly further, visit more trees, lay more nematode filled eggs and live longer than smaller ones.)

Once nematodes are well established in a sirex population, the parasitized female sirex perform the main task of spreading them. However, initially (where less than 1 percent of trees are naturally killed by sirex) the nematodes have to be introduced into new plantations by inoculating 'trap trees' set up at easily accessible strategic points. A group of 5 to 10 preferably low quality trees near the roadside are selected for each compartment (50 acres or so) a few months before the sirex flight season, and injected with just enough weedicide, so that they die slowly and are particularly attractive to sirex. Once sirex populations are established in these trap trees, the trees are felled and inoculated with nematodes, suspended in polyacrylamide gel, at a rate of 2000 per inoculation hole with holes about 1 cm deep and 30 cm apart.

Important factors are:

• Cutting the holes cleanly with a specially designed hammer/punch so that nematodes can easily enter the tracheids

• Using gel so that the nematodes are suspended within the hole for adequate time

• Introducing the nematodes when the wood is adequately moist

• Spacing of inoculation holes and number of nematodes introduced into each hole which has been carefully tested to provide maximum parasitism (over 98%) and minimum competition between fungal feeding nematodes and the fungal feeding sirex larvae so that the latter grow to full size (Bedding and Akhurst 1973)

• Because parasitized female sirex rarely leave the compartment of liberation it is important to introduce nematodes to each forest compartment and repeat inoculations, if required, each year until over 10 percent parasitism occurs in each compartment

Where sirex killed trees exceed 1 percent of the total, all naturally infested trees in every 5th row (20 percent) should be inoculated to achieve adequate control. Examples of successful treatment of sirex populations that were out of control because nematodes were not previously present are:

A) The Mt. Helen plantation in Tasmania in 1974 where 10 percent of all mature trees had been dying for each of the previous 6 years, all dead trees in every 10th row were inoculated. In 1975 there was near 100 percent parasitism and in 1976 there were negligible sirex.

B) The "Green Triangle" in South Australia/ Victoria in 1987 where there was up to 80 percent tree death in some areas, 166,000 sirex-killed trees (from every 5th row) were inoculated and by 1989 nearly 100 percent parasitism was followed by a population collapse; sirex has been rare in that region ever since (Haugen and Underdown 1990)

C) In a 12,000-ha plantation in Encruzilhado do Sul in Brazil, where sirex infested about 30 percent of trees in some compartments in

1991, nematodes were released from 1990 to 1993, resulting in levels of parasitism of 45 percent in 1991, 75 percent in 1992 and more than 90 percent in 1994. In 1995 it was difficult to find any sirex-infested trees in this area (Bedding and Iede 2005).

There has been one major problem with nematode control of sirex. Because *B. siricidicola* had been cultured in the free-living form for over 20 years without intervention of the parasitic life cycle, this led to the selection of a strain that rarely formed the pre-parasitic infective stage (Bedding and Iede 2005). Unfortunately the situation did not become apparent until this defective strain had been liberated for many years. However, in 1990 the original strain was re-isolated from where it had been liberated in Kamona, Tasmania in 1971 and stocks have been maintained since then in liquid nitrogen for re-establishment of the cultures used for all new introductions. In addition it has been found recently that even Kamona strain tends to deteriorate after several months of sub-culturing so that it is imperative to return to stocks stored in liquid nitrogen at least once at the beginning of each season. Nevertheless, replacing the defective strain in the field has proved very difficult particularly since it requires several back-crosses to the "Kamona" strain to completely revive infectivity. A program of strain replacement is still continuing in Australia aided by the development of RAPD molecular identification enabling separation of the defective and Kamona strains from field collected samples. Infectivity tests are also conducted on field collected samples by exposing acidic potato dextrose agar plates inoculated with *A. areolatum* and nematode eggs to an atmosphere containing 12 percent CO_2. (In this situation fewer than 10 percent of eggs from the defective strain give rise to parasitic females whereas over 80 percent of eggs from the Kamona strain do so.)

Now that *S. noctilio* has been found in both the USA and Canada it will be essential to use *B. siricidicola* to help protect the many millions of acres of highly susceptible pine there. Only top quality, Kamona strain nematodes should be used and their quality should be maintained using liquid nitrogen storage from the outset.

Literature Cited

Bedding, R.A. (1967) **Parasitic and free-living cycles in entomogenous nematodes of the genus *Deladenus***. Nature 214, 174–175.

Bedding, R.A. (1968) ***Deladenus wilsoni* n.sp. and *D. siricidicola* n.sp. (Neotylenchidae), entomophagous nematodes parasitic siricid woodwasps**. Nematologica **14, 515–525**.

Bedding, R.A. (1972) **Biology of *Deladenus siricidicola* (Neotylenchidae) an entomophagous nematode parasitic in siricid woodwasps**. Nematologica 18, 482–493.

Bedding, R.A. (1993) **Biological control of *Sirex noctilio* using the nematode *Deladenus siricidicola*.** In: Bedding, R.A., Akhurst, R.J. and Kaya, H.K. (eds) Nematodes and the Biological Control of Insect Pests. CSIRO publications, East Melbourne, Australia, pp. 11-20.

Bedding, R.A. and Akhurst, R.J. (1974) **Use of the nematode *Deladenus siricidicola* in the biological control of *Sirex noctilio* in Australia.** Journal of the Australian Entomological Society 13, 129–135.

Bedding, R.A. and Akhurst, R.J. (1978) **Geographical distribution and host preferences of *Deladenus* species (Nematoda: Neotylenchidae) parasitic in siricid woodwasps and associated hymenopterous parasitoids.** Nematologica 24, 286–294.

Bedding, R.A. and Iede, E.T. (2005) **Application of *Beddingia siricidicola* for Sirex Woodwasp Control**. In: Nematodes as Biological Control Agents (Editors Parwinder S. Grewal, Ralf-Udo Ehlers David I. Shapiro-Ilan) CABI Publishing 385:399.

Haugen, D.A. and Underdown, M.G. (1990) ***Sirex noctilio* control program in response to the 1987 Green Triangle outbreak**. Australian Forestry 53, 33–40.

Poinar, Jr, G.O., Jackson T.A., Bell, N.L. and Wahid, M.B. (2002) ***Elaeolenchus parthenonema* n. g. sp. (Nematoda: Sphaerularioidea: Anandeanematidae n. fam.) parasitic in the palm-pollinating weevil *Elaeidobius kamerunicus* Faust, with a phylogenetic synopsis of the Spherularioidea Lubbock, 1861.** Systematic Parasitology 52: 219-225.

TSUGA CHINENSIS AS A SOURCE OF HOST RESISTANCE
TO THE HEMLOCK WOOLLY ADELGID

S.E. Bentz[3], Robert J. Griesbach[2], Margaret R. Pooler[1] and A.M. Townsend[3]

USDA–ARS, U.S. National Arboretum, 3501 New York Ave., N.E, Washington, DC 20002[1]
10300 Baltimore Ave, Building 010A, BARC-W, Beltsville, MD 20705[2]
11601 Old Pond Drive, Glenn Dale, MD 20769[3]

ABSTRACT

The eastern North American native hemlock species, *T. canadensis* [L.] Carrière *and T. caroliniana* Engelm., are highly susceptible to injury from the hemlock woolly adelgid (HWA), while the Asian species, *T. chinensis* (Franch.) E. Pritz., *T. diversifolia* (Maxim.) Mast., and *T. sieboldii Carrière*, are reported to show more tolerance (McClure 1992, 1995). In western North America, the adelgid is not considered a pest problem, although it has been documented on the two native species, *T. mertensiana* (Bong.) Carrière and *T. heterophylla* (Raf.) Sarg. since the early 1900s. In Japan and China, HWA appears to be a relatively minor pest of *T. chinensis, T. diversifolia*, and *T. sieboldii* whose impact is limited by natural enemies, host resistance, and scattered distribution (McClure 1996, 1995, 1992, Montgomery 1999).

In the eastern U.S., resistance or tolerance by Asian species, most especially *T. chinensis*, has been supported by observation. No adelgids have been observed on the few *T. chinensis* and *T. diversifolia* at the U.S. National Arboretum for more than 10 years, although HWA infested trees are located in close proximity. At the Morris Arboretum in Philadelphia, adelgid has been observed on *T. diversifolia* but not on *T. chinensis* and recent plantings of *T. chinensis* at the Morris Arboretum are also thriving (M. Montgomery, personal communication). Similar occurrences were found at arboreta on the east coast of the United States in the early 1990s (R.J. Lewandowski, unpublished survey, personal communication). Recent research at the Arnold Arboretum examined tolerance to HWA and growth of *T. chinensis*. *T. chinensis* seedlings planted in a heavily HWA infested stand of *T. canadensis* were found to be completely free of HWA egg sacs and producing abundant new shoot growth in number and length after 4 years of exposure to HWA (Del Tredici and Kitajima 2004). For its resistance, plus shade tolerance and hardiness in USDA Zone 6, the authors found *T. chinensis* a suitable landscape alternative to *T. canadensis*.

The U.S. National Arboretum initiated a breeding program in the early 1990s to assess the potential for controlled hybridization among different hemlock species utilizing both susceptible eastern species and the Asian species *T. chinensis*, *T. diversifolia* and *T. sieboldii*. Attempts to hybridize *T. canadensis* with three Asiatic species were unsuccessful. However, more than 50 authentic hybrids from crosses between *T. caroliniana* and *T. chinensis* were identified by DNA fingerprinting. Hybrids were also identified from crosses between the *T. caroliniana* and *T. chinensis* and between the Asiatic species, *T. chinensis*, *T. diversifolia* and *T. sieboldii*. In 2002, the parents, their hybrids, and self-pollinated progeny were planted in a randomized block design at the USDA's South Farm, Beltsville, MD. Beginning in 2004, data collection began on important horticultural attributes of each tree including survival, growth rate, form, phenology, injury from cold, heat or pests, and evidence of natural adelgid infestation. Plants will be evaluated for adelgid resistance by artificial inoculation and data will be collected for such factors as plant growth, adelgid survival, number of ovisacs produced, number of eggs/ovisac, number of crawlers, and feeding injury. The research will be in cooperation with Michael E. Montgomery, USDA Forest Service, Center for Forest Health Research, Hamden, CT. The degree to which resistance, if observed, may be transferred from the Asian species into hybrid offspring, especially hybrids with the eastern North American species, will be of particular interest.

Because the Beltsville, MD location is outside the natural range of hemlock, propagation of hybrids to facilitate possible greenhouse studies of hybrids for HWA resistance and field testing in other geographic locations has also begun. Additionally, a field planting of 20 accessions of wild-collected *T. chinensis* and relatives were planted in 2004-2005 at the USDA's South Farm site. This germplasm includes accessions from two explorations to the People's Republic of China sponsored by the North American China Plant Exploration Committee (NACPEC) in 1996 and 1999. Accessions also represent regional and elevation variations which may affect the hardiness and/or suitability of *T. chinensis*. Trees in both hybrid and *T. chinensis* species plantings will be evaluated for form, hardiness, reproductive behavior and suitability for use in the forest or landscape.

Acknowledgments

This research was funded in part by USDA Forest Service Forest Health Technology Enterprise Team Agreement 11-2442-97-05 and RFP 2005 Interagency Agreement 05-IA-11242326-005.

Literature Cited

Bentz, S.E., L.G.H. Riedel, M.R. Pooler, and A.M. Townsend. 2002. **Hybridization and self-compatibility in controlled pollinations of eastern North American and Asian hemlock (*Tsuga*) species**. J. Arboriculture 28:200-205.

Del Tredici, Peter and Alice Kitajima. 2004. **Introduction and cultivation of Chinese hemlock (*Tsuga chinensis*) and its resistance to hemlock woolly adelgid (*Adelges tsugae*)**. Journal of Arboriculture: 30:282-287.

McClure, M.S. 1992. **Hemlock woolly adelgid**. American Nurseryman 175(6):82-89.

McClure, M.S. 1995. ***Diapterobates humeralis* agent of hemlock woolly adelgid (Homoptera: Adelgidae) in Japan**. Environmental Entomology 24(5):1207-1215.

McClure, M.S. 1996. **Woolly bully**. American Nurseryman 138(11):52-57.

Montgomery, Michael E. 1999. **Woolly adelgids in the Southern Appalachians: Why they are harmful and prospects for control. USDA Forest Health Technology Enterprise Team (FHTET-98-14)**. In: Proceedings of the Southern Appalachian Biological Control Initiative Workshop, September 26-27, 1996, pp 47-57.

Pooler, Margaret R. and LG.H. Riedel, S.E. Bentz, and A.M. Townsend. 2002. **Molecular markers used to verify interspecific hybridization between hemlock (*Tsuga*) species**. J. Amer. Soc. Hort. Sci. 127(4):623-627.

HOST RANGE OF THE EXOTIC BROWN MARMORATED STINK BUG, *HALYOMORPHA HALYS*, (HEMIPTERA: PENTATOMIDAE), IMPLICATIONS FOR FUTURE DISTRIBUTION

Gary Bernon[1], Karen M. Bernhard[2], Anne L. Nielsen[3], James F. Stimmel[4], E. Richard Hoebeke[5] and Maureen E. Carter[5]

[1]USDA APHIS Pest Survey, Detection, and Exclusion Lab., Otis ANGB, MA 02542
[2]Cooperative Extension, Lehigh County Agricultural Center, Allentown, PA 18104
[3]Department of Entomology, Rutgers University, New Brunswick, NJ 08901
[4]Pennsylvania Department of Agriculture, Harrisburg, PA 17110
[5]Department of Entomology, Cornell University, Ithaca, NY 14853

ABSTRACT

Halyomorpha halys, (Hemiptera: Pentatomidae), is a pest in eastern Asia on soybeans and woody plants, including broadleaved trees and fruit trees. A population was discovered in Allentown, PA in 2001. *H. halys* is also a nuisance pest as it overwinters in homes and other buildings. Based on earlier reports to the Lehigh County Extension in Allentown, the sting bug had been established since at least 1996.

H. halys is now reported throughout Pennsylvania and New Jersey; in 2003 a population was discovered in Hagerstown, MD. Specimens were found in 2004 in Delaware, West Virginia, and Virginia. An isolated population was reported in 2004 in Portland, OR, and four ornamental host plants were verified in 2005. Preliminary analysis of mitochondrial DNA suggested only one maternal haplotype in the United States. However, analysis of specimens from potential source populations in Asia as well as from isolated populations in the United States will have to be completed to show a conclusive pattern (Carter, unpublished data).

Host plant surveys indicated that *H. halys* is polyphagous with patchy and sometimes dense populations, but limited to landscaped urban areas. Damage to fruit trees and feeding on vegetables was observed in gardens. Until populations reach commercial growers, population dynamics in agro-ecosystems will not be apparent. Woody plants including ornamentals and trees are primary hosts in urban landscaped areas. However, in Pennsylvania, a population was observed in 2005 to invade a soybean field, and as host range expands south, pest populations on soybeans and fruit trees are likely to occur. Also, populations were univoltine in Pennsylvania, however that is likely to change with southern range expansion, increasing the potential for crop damage.

A MODEL FOR THE OPTIMIZATION OF THE DETECTION AND ERADICATION OF ISOLATED GYPSY MOTH COLONIES

Tiffany L. Bogich[1], Andrew Liebhold[2] and Katriona Shea[1]

[1]The Pennsylvania State University, IGDP in Ecology and Department of Biology
208 Mueller Laboratory, University Park, PA 16802

[2]USDA Forest Service, Northeastern Research Station
180 Canfield St., Morgantown, WV 26505-3180

ABSTRACT

Biological invasions of pest species pose a threat to the stability of ecosystems, both natural and managed (Liebhold et al. 1995, Shogren and Tschirhart 2005). Considerable effort is expended by national and local governments on excluding alien species via detection and eradication of invading populations, but these efforts are not necessarily designed in the most economically or biologically efficient manner. In places where an invasive species has not yet established, we need to know how managers can optimize detection methods in order to minimize both detection and eradication costs.

Practical limitations that constrain the detection and management of small, newly founded alien populations are common problems for managers (Welk 2004). Early detection is one of the most cost-effective ways to reduce the impact of invasive species worldwide (Myers et al. 2000, Byers et al. 2002, U.S. National Invasive Species Council 2005). Therefore, there is an urgent need to design and test monitoring strategies in order to achieve early detection and, in turn, provide more effective control (Ruckelshaus et al. 2002).

Using the North American gypsy moth (*Lymantria dispar*) as a case study, we develop a mathematical model to consider the trade-offs between increased detection costs associated with high detection efforts (i.e. high trap densities) and decreased eradication costs due to the ability to detect populations when they are smaller and less expensive to control. We develop a mathematical model to aid in the trapping design both for detection and eradication efforts in the western and midwestern U.S. and for Slow-the-Spread management activities along the northeastern edge of the U.S.

We chose the ongoing invasion of the gypsy moth in North America because of the availability of extensive life history survey data describing its spread and because of prior research to examine various methods to slow that spread. The gypsy moth continues to slowly expand its range across North America from the site of its initial introduction in Massachusetts; it is considered a significant threat to both natural and managed systems. Gypsy moth outbreaks often result in defoliation of vast expanses of forests. Over 300 million acres of forested land and urban and rural treed areas in the United States were identified as at risk for gypsy moth invasion in 1995 (U.S. Department of Agriculture).

We use mathematical models to determine the optimal trapping densities with respect to minimizing management costs and maximizing the ability to detect new gypsy moth infestations. The implicitly spatial model considers a generally infested area in which variable densities of traps are randomly distributed in a finite area, in order to detect colonies that are also randomly distributed. We examine the effect of several parameters including arrival rate, colony growth rate, total area, and cost on the optimal trap density.

Because the rate of new colony arrival and establishment is highly variable in nature and depends on several ecological and social factors (including forest type, human population density, transportation infrastructure, and climate,), we specifically examine the case of low and high colony arrival and establishment rates. Initial results indicate that as arrival and establishment rates increase, the optimal density of traps needed to minimize cost and maximize detection abilities increases also, but much less rapidly than expected.

In the future, we plan to further investigate the impact of trapping design on minimizing cost and maximizing the ability to detect new colonies through the use of spatially explicit models and Monte Carlo simulation techniques. Additionally, all of these models will be useful in designing monitoring strategies, not only for the gypsy moth, but also for other invasive forest pests.

Literature Cited

Byers, J. E. et al. (2002). **"Directing Research to Reduce the Impacts of Nonindigenous Species."** Conservation Biology 16(3): 630-640.

Liebhold, A. M. et al. (1995). **"Invasion by exotic forest pests: a threat to forest ecosystems."** Forest Science Monographs 30: 49.

Myers, J. H. et al. (2000). **"Eradication revisited: dealing with exotic species."** Trends in Ecology & Evolution 15(8): 316-320.

Ruckelshaus, M. H. et al. (2002). **"The Pacific salmon wars: What science brings to the challenge of recovering species."** Annual Review of Ecology and Systematics 33: 665-706.

Shogren, J. F. and T. Tschirhart (2005). **"Integrating ecology and economics to address bioinvasions."** Ecological Economics 52(3): 267-271.

U.S. Department of Agriculture (1995). **"Gypsy moth management in the United States: a cooperative approach."** Final Environmental Impact Statement.

U.S. National Invasive Species Council (2005). **"Progress Report on the Meeting the Invasive Species Challenge: National Invasive Species Management Plan."**

Welk, E. (2004). **"Constraints in range predictions of invasive plant species due to non-equilibrium distribution patterns: Purple loosestrife (*Lythrum salicaria*) in North America."** Ecological Modelling 179(4): 551-567.

A COMPARISON OF STRATEGIES FOR EXPERIMENTALLY INOCULATING EASTERN HEMLOCK WITH THE HEMLOCK WOOLLY ADELGID

Elizabeth Butin[1], Evan Preisser[1] and Joseph Elkinton[1]

[1]University of Massachusetts at Amherst, Amherst, MA

ABSTRACT

We assessed the importance of several factors potentially affecting the settlement rate of the invasive hemlock woolly adelgid, *Adelges tsugae*, on uninfested foliage of the eastern hemlock, *Tsuga canadensis*. We conducted our experiments in Massachusetts (USA) with overwintering sistens adelgids, and applied standard densities of infested foliage to uninfested branches in a planned multiple-comparison design. Settlement rates of progrediens crawlers produced by the overwintering sistens were highest when adelgid-infested foliage was loosely attached to uninfested foliage and both branches were then enclosed in a mesh sleeve. Early-emerging crawlers settled at a higher rate than did late-emerging crawlers. Increasing the density of infested branches did not affect settlement rates. We also tested whether less severe winter conditions improved settlement. There was no effect of using adelgids from more southern locations, and overwintering infested foliage in a refrigerator decreased settlement rate relative to foliage overwintered outdoors; however, methodological issues may have confounded both experiments. Our results suggest the following protocol for adelgid inoculations: (1) Time the inoculation to coincide with the beginning of crawler emergence from infested foliage; (2) Use a waterpic to keep infested foliage alive longer; (3) Loosely attach the infested foliage to the target branch, and enclose both branches in a mesh sleeve; and (4) Use the overwintering, high-fecundity sistens generation to maximize the number of emerging crawlers. Using a protocol like the one described above could substantially increase the success rate of experimental manipulations and encourage additional research on the population dynamics of this pest.

HISTORY AND MANAGEMENT OF SIREX WOOD WASP IN AUSTRALIA

Angus J. Carnegie

Forest Resources Research, NSW Department of Primary Industries,
PO Box 100 Beecroft NSW 2119, Australia

ABSTRACT

Introduction

This paper reviews the history and management of *Sirex noctilio* in Australia, including information from previous reviews as well as more recent data. The sirex wood wasp, *Sirex noctilio*, is one of the most important insect pests of *Pinus radiata* in Australia. Native to Europe, North Africa and Turkey, *S. noctilio* was introduced accidentally into Tasmania and detected there in 1951 (Neumann & Minko 1981). It then spread to the mainland and was detected in Victoria in 1961, and southern New South Wales (NSW) and South Australia by 1980 (Neumann & Minko 1981, Eldridge & Simpson 1987, Eldridge & Taylor 1989, Morgan 1989, Haugen et al. 1990, Haugen 1990). Sirex has not been detected in Queensland or Western Australia, although susceptible hosts grow in these states.

The biology and behaviour of *S. noctilio* has been detailed previously (Morgan & Stewart 1966, Taylor 1978, 1981; Neumann & Minko 1981, Madden 1988). Briefly, eggs are oviposited into trees which have low sap pressure, along with a phytotoxic mucus and a wood decay fungus (*Amylostereum areolatum*) carried by the wasps. Trees drilled by sirex soon die due to the combination of the mucus and fungus.

Sirex outbreaks in Australia

The significant pest status of sirex was soon realized once the wasp had established in the southern states of Australia. In Tasmania, up to 40 percent of intermediate-age slow-growing *P. radiata* in an area of 1,100 -ha near Hobart were destroyed within 6 years of the first record (Madden 1975, 1998). In Victoria, about 25 percent of a 1,900-ha plantation at Delatite in

central Victoria was damaged by sirex, with over 70 percent damaged in intermediate-age unthinned stands over a 7-year period (Neumann & Minko 1981). In the 'Green Triangle' (southeastern South Australia and southwestern Victoria) over 1.8 million trees were killed in a single year (1987), 7 years after detection of sirex in the region (Haugen 1990; Haugen & Underdown 1990; Madden 1998). In Hume Region, NSW, between 1987 and 1989, approximately 15 percent of 1,200 ha of unthinned stands were killed by sirex (Carnegie et al. 2005). In Macquarie Region, also in NSW, approximately 30 percent of 1,000 ha of unthinned stands were killed between 1991 and 1992 (Carnegie et al. 2005).

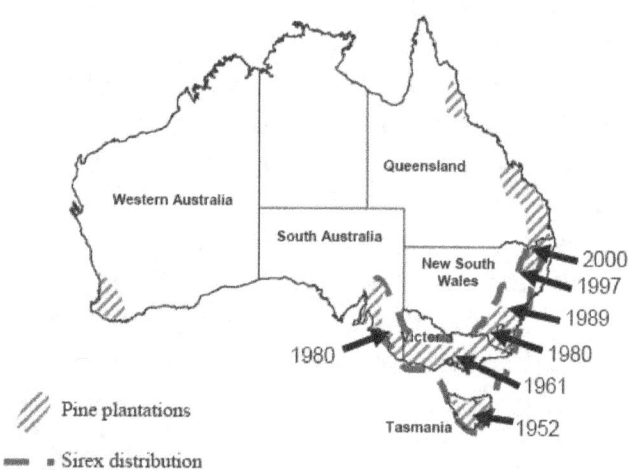

Figure 1. Map of Australia with location of exotic *Pinus* plantations (hatched) and distribution of sirex (dashed line), including the years sirex was detected in various regions in Australia.

Management of sirex in Australia

Control of sirex is achieved by the use of a combination of silvicultural and biological measures (Neumann et al. 1987, Eldridge & Taylor 1989, Morgan 1989, Haugen et al. 1990), as well as regular monitoring and forest health surveillance (Haugen et al. 1990, National Sirex Coordination Committee 2005).

30 *Proceedings—Interagency Research Forum on Gypsy Moth and other Invasive Species*

Monitoring and surveillance

Determine sirex levels in areas of known infestation.—Where sirex is known to be in an area, surveys are used to determine the levels of infestation to identify further management options.

1. Aerial surveys, mostly by helicopter, are used as an initial step to identify the extent and incidence of dead trees (with typical symptoms of sirex attack). The majority of exotic *Pinus* plantations in Australia are surveyed annually.

2. Ground surveys are then used as a follow-up to confirm the causal agent of dead trees. These can also identify whether sirex has attacked suppressed trees that are often difficult to identify from the air.

3. Trap trees are mainly used in Australia as part of the biological control program (see below), but can also be used to identify very low levels of sirex.

4. Insect traps, using lures (alpha- and beta-pinene) have been used in recent years where sirex is at very low levels and cannot be detected either in trap trees or aerial and ground surveys.

Detection in areas not known to have sirex

Where sirex it not known to be in an area, the above monitoring and surveillance techniques are also used to increase the chance of detection.

Silvicultural methods.—Silvicultural treatment is concerned with maintaining the health and vigor of trees and minimizing water stress, with healthy pine trees resulting from such treatment very resistant to attack by sirex wasps (Haugen 1990, Eldridge & Taylor 1989). By managing plantations optimally (e.g., timing selective thinning to sustain tree vigor, restricting pruning and thinning to waste outside the wasp flight season and maintaining hygiene in the plantation through early felling of dying or diseased trees) the risk to pine plantations from sirex attack can be greatly reduced. However, market forces and/or budgetary constraints result in delayed thinning in many instances resulting in stressed stands.

Biological control.— Even with good plantation management, factors outside human control, such as prolonged drought, can predispose whole plantations to sirex infestation. For this reason it is essential to implement biological control measures. Selected parasites have been imported into Australia from Europe and North America to assist in the control of sirex. The most effective of these is the nematode *Beddingia* (=*Deladenus*) *siricidicola* (Neotylenchidae), which feeds on the sirex fungus (*A. areolatum*) in one phase of its life history and infects sirex larvae in the other phase (Bedding 1967, 1972, 1993; Bedding & Akhurst 1974; Neumann & Minko 1981; Eldridge & Taylor 1989; Morgan 1989; Haugen et al. 1990). Infected sirex larvae complete their development into adult wasps but, because of nematode infection, the resulting female wasps are sterile. Several parasitic wasps were also introduced into Australia to help control sirex, including *Ibalia leucospoides* (Ibaliidae), *Megarhyssa nortoni* (Ichneumonidae) and two species of *Rhyssa* (Ichneumonidae) (Neumann & Minko 1981, Eldridge & Taylor 1989, Morgan 1989, Haugen et al. 1990).

Trap trees are used to assist in the introduction of nematodes into the sirex population. A network of trees are poisoned and made attractive to sirex during flight season. Once sirex larvae are detected in these trees, they are inoculated with the nematode. Billets (bolts) are cut from trap trees and monitored for parasitism rates to help in evaluating the biological control agents. Further detail on the nematode inoculation program can be found in National Sirex Coordination Committee (2005) and Haugen et al. (1990).

Conclusion

Although sirex can be a devastating pest of exotic pine plantations, effective management has now significantly reduced its impact in Australia.

Acknowledgments

The author would like to thank the members of the (Australian) National Sirex Coordination Committee for sharing their knowledge and expertise, and USDA/APHIS/PPQ for the financial support to attend the meeting, and especially Vic Maestro and Dave Williams.

References

Bedding, R.A. (1967). **Parasitic and free-living cycles in entomogenous nematodes of the genus** *Deladenus*. Nature (London) 214: 174-5.

Bedding, R.A. (1972). **Biology of** *Deladenus siricidicola* **(Neotylenchidae) an entomophagous nematode parasitic in siricid woodwasps.** Nematologica 18: 482-93.

Bedding, R.A. (1993) **Biological Control of** *Sirex noctilio* **using the nematode** *Deladenus siricidicola*. *In:* **Nematodes and the biological control of insect pests (Eds R.A. Bedding, R.J. Akhurst & H.K. Kaya)** CSIRO Publications 11-20.

Bedding, R.A. and Akhurst, R.J. (1974). **Use of the nematode** *Deladenus siricidicola* **in the biological control of** *Sirex noctilio* **in Australia.** Journal of the Australian Entomological Society 13: 129-35.

Carnegie, A. J., Matsuki, M., Hurley, B.P., Ahumada, R., Haugen, D.A., Klasmer, P., Jianghua Sun & Iede, E.T. (2006). **Predicting the potential distribution of** *Sirex noctilio* **(Hymenoptera: Siricidae), a significant exotic pest of** *Pinus* **plantations.** Annals of Forest Science 63, 119-128.

Carnegie, A. J., Eldridge, R. H. And Waterson, D. G. (2005). **The history and management of sirex wood wasp,** *Sirex noctilio* **(Hymenoptera: Siricidae), In: New South Wales, Australia.** New Zealand Journal of Forestry Science 35, 3 24.

Eldridge, R.H.; Simpson, J.A. 1987: **Development of contingency plans for use against exotic pests and diseases of trees and timber. 3. Histories of control measures against some introduced pests and diseases of forests and forest products in Australia.** Australian Forestry 50: 24-36.

Eldridge, R.H.; Taylor, E.E. 1989: *Sirex* **woodwasp—a pest of pine in N.S.W.** Forestry Commission of N.S.W. Forest Protection Series No. 1.5 pp.

Haugen, D.A.; Underdown, G. 1990: *Sirex noctilio* **program in response to the 1987 Green Triangle outbreak.** Australian Forestry 53: 33-40.

Haugen, D.A. 1990: **Control procedures for** *Sirex noctilio* **in the Green Triangle: Review from detection to severe outbreak (1977-1987).** Australian Forestry 53: 24-32.

Haugen, D.A.; Bedding, R.A.; Underdown, M.G.; Neumann, F.G. 1990: **National strategy for control of** *Sirex noctilio* **in Australia.** Australian Forest Grower 13: Special Liftout Section No. 13. 8 pp.

Madden, J.L. 1975: **An analysis of an outbreak of the woodwasp** *Sirex noctilio* **F. (Hymenoptera:** *Siricidae*), *In:* *Pinus radiata*. Bulletin of Entomological Research 65: 491-500.

Madden, J.L. 1988: **Sirex in Australasia.** *In:* **Dynamics of forest insect populations. A. A. Berryman (Ed).** Plenum Publishing, NY. pp 407-429.

Morgan, F.D.; Stewart, N.C. 1966: **The biology and behaviour of the woodwasp** *Sirex noctilio* **(F.) In New Zealand.** Transaction of the Royal Society of New Zealand 7: 195-204.

Morgan, F.D. 1989: **Forty years of** *Sirex noctilio* **and** *Ips grandicollis* **in Australia.** New Zealand Journal of Forestry Science 19: 198-209.

National Sirex Co-ordination Committee 2005: **National Sirex Control Strategy,** Operations Worksheet No. 1.

Neumann, F.G.; Minko, G. 1981: **The sirex wood wasp in Australian** *radiata* **pine plantations.** Australian Forestry 44: 46-63.

Neumann, F.G.; Motey, J.L.; Mckimm, R.J. 1987: **The sirex wasp in Victoria.** Department Bulletin No. 29: 44 pp.

Taylor, K.L. 1978: **Evaluation of the insect parasitoids of** *Sirex noctilio* **(Hymenoptera:** Siricidae*) in Tasmania.** Oeocologia 32, 1-10.

Taylor, K.L. 1981: **The Sirex woodwasp: ecology and control of an introduced forest insect. In: The Ecology of Pests (eds) R.L. Kitching and R.E. Jones.** CSIRO, Australia, pp 231-248.

MULTI-YEAR RESIDUAL ACTIVITY OF ARBORJET'S IMA-JET (IMIDACLOPRID 5% SL) AGAINST EMERALD ASH BORER [*AGRILUS PLANIPENNIS* FAIREMAIRE (COLEOPTERA: BUPRESTIDAE)] IN GREEN ASH (*FRAXINUS PENNSYLVANICA* MARSH) IN TROY, MI.

Joseph J. Doccola, Peter M. Wild, Eric J. Bristol, Joseph Lojko and Xin Li

ABSTRACT

In cooperative university studies, IMA-jet treated green ash were effectively protected for 2 years to date in Troy, MI against emerald ash borer (EAB). Trees were infested at the time of treatment, exhibiting epicormic sprouting and thinning canopies. Twenty trees were injected with IMA-jet alone or with a diluent to aid uptake and translocation within the vascular tissues. Using Arborjet's Tree I.V., the 5 percent formulation of imidacloprid was delivered into the sapwood at a rate of 8mL/DBH for trees 12-23 inches in diameter. In the spring 2004 study, Onyx and BotaniGard treatments were applied as sprays. The other systemic insecticide treatments were either orthene (AceCap) or imidacloprid (Merit 75 drench or Mauget Imicide). AceCap is applied as a trunk implant, and Imicide as a stem microinjection. Extent of larval mortality and galleries were based on assessments of bark scraping three 5 cm caliper limbs per tree. Treatment means were separated by ANOVA LSD at $P < 0.05$. Six treatments had a density of new galleries significantly less than the controls. Of these, the two Arborjet treatments had the lowest density of new galleries (0–1.2/ m^2). The Arborjet IMA-jet trunk injection treatments provided a high level of control (92 –100%), suggesting efficacy against 2nd-year as well as 1st-year larvae. Canopy assessments were conducted in the fall 2005, 495 days after treatment. Control trees or other treatments had intact canopies of between 0-20 percent. Arborjet treated IMA-jet trees had mean canopy densities of 80 percent suggesting multiyear residual activity. Larval mortality and gallery densities are presently being evaluated for year two efficacy. The diluent is now incorporated into IMA-jet's formulation to enhance uptake.

SEMIOCHEMICALS PROVIDE A DETERRENT TO THE BLACK TWIG BORER, *XYLOSANDRUS COMPACTUS* (COLEOPTERA: CURCULIONIDAE, SCOLYTINAE)

Nick Dudley[1], John D. Stein[2], Tyler Jones[1] and Nancy Gillette[3]

[1]Hawaii Agricultural Research Center, Aiea, HI 96701

[2]USDA Forest Service, Forest Health Technology Enterprise Team, Morgantown, WV 26505

[3]USDA Forest Service, Pacific Southwest Research Station, Berkeley, CA 94701

ABSTRACT

The black twig borer (*Xylosandrus compactus*) (BTB) is a serious pest of agriculture, forestry, and native Hawaiian plants. The BTB is a typical ambrosia beetle that bores into the host and inoculates the galleries with an ambrosia fungus (*Fusarium solani*) known to cause cankers, root rot, and wilt. The host list for this beetle is extensive and contains several Hawaiian plant species listed as threatened and endangered. Our approach focused on reforestation of koa plantations, one of the most important of these host species in terms of cultural and economic values, to evaluate attractants and repellants to help monitor, control, or prevent BTB damage.

We had earlier demonstrated that ethanol-baited Japanese beetle traps were an effective means of trapping BTB, so we used that trap/bait combination as the positive control. This system also effectively trapped two nontarget scolytid pest species, the Asian ambrosia beetle (*Xylosandrus crassiusculus*) and the fruit-tree pinhole borer (*Xyleborinus saxeseni*).

We challenged the attraction of the ethanol trapping system using both verbenone and limonene as effective repellents. The study was located in a 6-year-old *Acacia koa* forest restoration stand, in Maunawili Valley on the windward side of the island of Oahu, with high BTB populations and considerable BTB-caused mortality. Treatments, each replicated six times, consisted of ethanol-baited control traps, ethanol and verbenone, and ethanol and limonene. Eighteen traps were placed in a grid at 15 m intervals and were suspended 1.5 m above the ground. Traps were monitored for 4 weeks, with collections made on a weekly basis. Trap counts were analyzed with generalized linear models for over-dispersed Poisson-distributed responses. Multiple comparisons were based on the maximum likelihood ratio.

Verbenone significantly reduced trap catch of all three beetle species. Limonene significantly reduced trap catch for only the Asian ambrosia beetle. Future work will utilize a higher release system for verbenone. Positive results will be applied to other tree species, with particular emphasis on restoration of endangered species in the state of Hawaii.

DEVELOPMENT OF A NEW RISK ASSESSMENT PROCEDURE FOR PINEWOOD NEMATODE IN EUROPE

Hugh F. Evans, Sam Evans and Makihiko Ikegami

Forest Research, Alice Holt Lodge, Farnham, Surrey, GU10 4LH, UK

ABSTRACT

Research, partly funded under the EU PHRAME (Plant Health Risk And Monitoring Evaluation) program has provided new information on the biology and ecology of pinewood nematode (PWN), *Bursaphelenchus xylophilus*, in Portugal. Studies have been carried out by eight partner research teams in six countries (UK—coordinator, Austria, France, Germany, Portugal, Spain). Data gathered have improved our understanding of the interaction of PWN, its vectors and host trees in both a European and a global context. Specifically, *Monochamus galloprovincialis*, has taken on the role of vector in Portugal and results have indicated that it has a single generation a year with a well-defined flight period. Collection of strains of *B. xylophilus* and their mass culture has enabled biological and molecular studies to be carried out, suggesting that there are two strains of the nematode in Portugal. Detailed studies of early infestation of seedling trees in both Germany and Portugal have provided excellent information on rapid movement of nematodes in the tree, followed by onset of wilt symptoms. Data from all partners are being incorporated in a new risk model based on existing process-based models of tree growth developed in the UK. These are driven by the differences between actual and potential transpiration in host trees and the interactions with site, temperature, moisture regimes and presence of nematodes in the tree. Predictions from the new models are being tested using parameters from the known infested area of Portugal. This new approach should allow refined assessment of the likelihood of wilt expression both in Europe and internationally.

Background to the PHRAME program

Pinewood nematode (PWN), *Bursaphelenchus xylophilus* (Nematoda: Aphelchoididae), is native to North America where it exists primarily in a saprophytic mode linked closely to the oviposition activities of vectors in the genus *Monochamus* (Coleoptera: Cerambycidae). Nematodes will also enter the tree through maturation feeding wounds made by adult *Monochamus*. Under certain conditions, thought to be mainly driven by high summer temperatures and availability of susceptible tree species, trees can exhibit rapid wilting symptoms followed by early mortality. This is rare in North America, but has been highly prevalent when the nematode has established in new regions, notably in Japan, China, Korea and, from 1999, in Portugal. In each new situation the local species of *Monochamus* has taken on the role of vector and in most cases have proved highly effective in transmission of nematodes from tree to tree, usually at local scales.

Although there have been studies of how *B. xylophilus* compromises the vascular system of host trees resulting in loss of water flow in the xylem, cavitation and wilt expression, it has not been possible to determine precisely how the nematode results in such rapid effects, even on large mature trees.

The EU research program PHRAME (Plant Health Risk And Monitoring Evaluation) has addressed the whole spectrum of interactions between PWN, its vectors and tree susceptibility in the context of the recent establishment of the nematode in Portugal. The partnership involved is indicated in the following table:

Principal scientist	Institute	E-mail/web page
H. F. Evans	Forest Research, Farnham, UK	hugh.evans@forestry.gsi.gov.uk http://www.forestresearch.gov.uk/fr/INFD-63KGEF
T. Schröder	BBA/AG, Braunschweig, Germany	t.schroeder@BBA.DE http://www.bba.de/english/bbaeng.htm
M. M. Mota	Dept of Biology, U of Evora, Portugal	mmota@uevora.pt http://www.dbio.uevora.pt/
M. Arias (Now retired)	CSIC, Madrid, Spain	maria.arias@ccma.csic.es http://www.ccma.es/dpts/agro/agro1.htm
C. Tomiczek	BFW, Vienna, Austria	christian.tomiczek@bfw.gv.at http://bfw ac at
W. Burgermeister	BBA/PS, Braunschweig, Germany	w.bergermeister@bba.de http://www.bba.de/english/bbaeng htm
P. Castagnone-Sereno	INRA, Antibes, France	pca@antibes.inra.fr http://www.antibes.inra.fr/ipmsv/index.en.html
E. Sousa	INIA, Oeiras, Portugal	Edmundo.Sousa@efn.com.pt http://www.efn.com.pt/

More detailed information on the Work Packages within the program can be found on the consortium website: *http://www.forestresearch.gov.uk/fr/INFD-63KGEF.* The key findings from research carried out since the program started in February 2003 are summarized here. Contact with the respective partners should be made if further information is required on particular topics.

Vector identification and biology

Within Portugal, Edmundo Sousa and colleagues, have studied PWN infested trees and have examined a wide range of bark and wood-boring beetles associated with those trees. Although many beetle species had colonized the trees, the only insect known to be an effective vector of PWN was *Monochamus galloprovincialis*, which is found in several European countries. Emergence commences in mid-May and is usually complete by late August; flight periods extend this by up to 1 month. Within the known PWN-infested area, up to 75 percent of *M. galloprovincialis* captured in traps were found to carry nematodes. However, surveys by Maria Arias and colleagues in Spain did not detect any *B. xylophilus* in the *M. galloprovincialis*. Feeding activity by *Monochamus galloprovincialis pistor* was studied by Christian Tomiczek and co-workers in Austria. Feeding was greatest in the first 2 weeks after emergence and the adults showed preferences for cut branches compared with whole seedling trees. This rapid early feeding phase is also coincident with the peak of nematode transmission by the beetles (Edmundo Sousa).

Surveys have provided collections of a range of *Bursaphelenchus* species and these have been categorized and many are now in culture collections maintained by Manuel Mota in Portugal. This valuable resource is providing material for molecular analysis of the variation in different populations of *B. xylophilus* which is being carried out by Wolfgang Burgermeister in Germany and Philippe Castagnon-Sereno in France. RAPD and satellite DNA techniques are being used in a complementary fashion to determine the phylogeny of the strains of nematodes present in Portugal. This will provide information to help determine the likely origin and pathway of entry of nematodes to Europe.

Work by Sam Evans and Makihiko Ikegami in the UK is concentrating on novel methods for assessing the likelihood of wilt expression in trees where the nematode has been introduced by maturation feeding. The basis for this approach

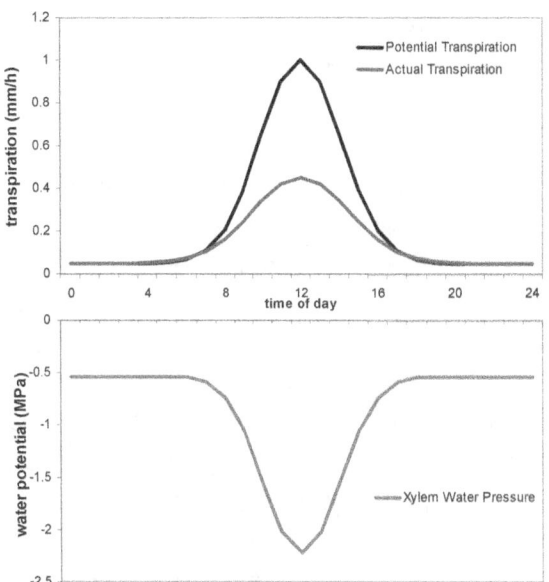

Figure 1: The difference between potential transpiration and actual transpiration expressed as xylem pressure (MPa).

is to employ process-based models of tree growth that have already been developed by staff at our institute. The key variables are those related to potential and actual transpiration by the host tree. This is illustrated in Figure 1, where the difference between potential and actual transpiration is expressed as xylem pressure in increasingly negative MPa (megapascals).

As water demand rises in a situation where water supply is constant the xylem pressure increases (greater negative value) and there is a risk of cavitation in xylem vessels. In most situations trees will reduce the deficit by reducing transpiration through stomatal closure during peak demand when the plant is photosynthesising in daylight. Recovery, even from quite severe reductions in xylem pressure and potential cavitation usually takes place during the hours of darkness. However, when PWN is present some of the xylem vessels are irreversibly blocked and this compromises the ability of the tree to recover from episodes of high-negative xylem pressure. The process based models of tree growth have been adapted to simulate the presence of PWN under a range of eco-climatic conditions. Current simulations have included (i) normal temperatures and water availability;

(ii) higher than average temperatures but normal water availability; and (iii) reduced water availability but normal temperatures all with and without the presence of PWN. Early indications from simulations runs of the model are that high temperature conditions, with normal water availability tend to result in onset of irreversible cavitation and onset of wilt expression. Interestingly, high temperatures, but higher than normal water availability, did not result in irreversible wilt, even though there was a sharp decline in xylem pressure. Similarly, low water availability (drought conditions) but normal temperatures did not always result in irreversible wilt; we speculate that under low water availability this is due to effective shutting down of transpiration and under high water availability water uptake can compensate for all levels of transpiration.

We are now exploring a wider range of parameters to test the models and also including the exploitation of carbon by the tree, with a particular view to simulating how the tree apportions and subsequently employs carbon for either growth or storage/defence. Early results suggest that apart from immediate effects of water availability, there may be carry-over effects on carbon usage that could compromise early growth and bud burst in the spring following nematode infestation in the previous summer or autumn.

Future Work

Although the new process-based models offer a novel procedure for assessing risks based on input of eco-climatic parameters, they still need to be verified in a field situation. This work is likely to be carried out during 2006 when field inoculation with PWN will be carried out on 10-year-old trees in Portugal and detailed measurements of a range of physiological parameters relevant to the input criteria for the models will be carried out. These data will be used to improve the models and to extend their use to refine the Pest Risk Analysis for PWN in Europe and globally.

Acknowledgments

Thanks are due to the partners in this consortium for excellent collaboration and for agreeing to allow some of their data to be presented at the meeting in Annapolis. We acknowledge the financial support from the European Union under the Framework Programme 5 project QLK5-CT-2002-00672. Hugh Evans would also like to thank USDA Forest Service and Kathy McManus in particular for assistance in enabling him to attend the meeting.

AN *OPHIOSTOMA* SP. CAUSING A VASCULAR WILT DISEASE OF RED BAY (*PERSEA BORBONIA* [L.] SPRENG) IS ALSO PATHOGENIC TO OTHER SPECIES IN THE LAURACEAE FAMILY

Stephen Fraedrich

USDA Forest Service, Southern Research Station, 320 Green St., Athens, GA 30602

ABSTRACT

Extensive mortality of red bay (*Persea borbonia* [L.] Spreng) has been observed in the coastal plains of South Carolina and Georgia since 2003. Dead and dying trees exhibit wilt-like symptoms, and a fungus (an *Ophiostoma* sp.) and an exotic ambrosia beetle (*Xyleborus glabratus* [Eichhoff]) have been implicated in the disease. Additional information about this disease is provided by Rabaglia and Fraedrich (this proceedings). Sassafras (*Sassafras albidum* [Nutt.] Nees) mortality was also observed at several sites in Georgia during the spring of 2005. Wilted sassafras exhibited sapwood discoloration, and *X. glabratus* and the *Ophiostoma* sp. were also associated with these trees.

The objective of this study was to evaluate the susceptibility of sassafras, red bay, swamp red bay (*P. palustris* [Raf.] Sarg.) and spicebush (*Lindera benzoin* [L.] Blume) to wilt caused by the *Ophiostoma* sp. Ten plants of each plant species were wounded and inoculated with drops of conidial suspensions of the *Ophiostoma* sp. Five control plants of each species were also wounded and inoculated with drops of sterile water. Plants were placed in a growth chamber, and observations of disease progression were made periodically. After 5 weeks, the sapwood of all plants was evaluated for discoloration, and samples from plants were plated on a media selective for the *Ophiostoma* sp.

Spicebush, sassafras, swamp red bay as well as red bay were all susceptible to wilt caused by the *Ophiostoma* sp. All plants inoculated with the *Ophiostoma* sp. wilted within 2 to 5 weeks. Sapwood discoloration was noted in plants of all species inoculated with the *Ophiostoma* isolates, and the *Ophiostoma* sp. was reisolated from these plants. Based on the results of this study, and recent observations of the wilt on sassafras in Georgia, there is reason to be concerned that the disease could affect other plant species. Additional species of Lauraceae in the southeast include pondberry (*Lindera melissifolia* [Walt.] Blume) and pondspice (*Litsea aestivalis* [L.] Fernald), which are both listed as endangered or threatened plants. Other species in the Lauraceae are common components of forests in other areas of the United States and neighboring countries.

EFFECTS OF HOST SPECIES AND POPULATION DENSITY ON *ANOPLOPHORA GLABRIPENNIS* FLIGHT PROPENSITY

Joseph A. Francese[1], David R. Lance[1], Baode Wang[1], Zhichun Xu[2], Alan J. Sawyer[1] and Victor C. Mastro[1]

[1]USDA APHIS PPQ Otis Pest Survey Detection and Exclusion Laboratory, Bldg 1398, Otis ANGB, MA 02542

[2]Beijing Forestry University, College of Biological Sciences and Technology, Haidin, Beijing, China 100083

ABSTRACT

Anoplophora glabripennis Motschulsky (Coleoptera: Cerambycidae), the Asian longhorned beetle (ALB) is a pest of hardwoods in its native range of China. While the host range of this pest has been studied extensively, its mechanisms for host selection are still unknown. Our goal was to study the factors influencing movement and orientation of adult ALB in order to determine if beetle behavior can be exploited to enhance survey and control efforts. Studies were performed near Qintongxia, Ningxia A.R., P.R. of China using potted trees. In 2002, Chinese (*Populus alba* and *P. nigra* var. *thevestina*) and American hosts (*Acer platanoides* and *A. saccharum*) were compared with an artificial tree. Marked beetles were observed hourly, and an exponential decay model ($y = e^{-\beta t}$; where β represented the rate of departure from hosts) was fit to the data. ALB remained on the North American maples to the Chinese poplars and the artificial tree. In 2004, a similar study was conducted with an Asian maple host, *A. mono*, *P. nigra*, *A. platanoides* and an artificial tree. Significantly more ALB remained on the maples than on the poplar or the artificial tree, but there was no significant difference in retention on the maples. In 2005, we wanted to determine if population density played a role in ALB flight propensity. We placed ALB adults in one of four groups on potted *P. nigra* var. *thevestina*: 2/tree, 4/tree, 8/tree and 16/tree. Again, marked beetles were observed hourly, and an exponential decay model ($y = e^{-\beta t}$; where β represented the rate of departure from hosts) was fit to the data. While there was no difference in the 4/tree, 8/tree and 16/tree groups, ALB in these three groups were more likely to fly than those in the 2/tree group.

EFFECTS OF TRAP DESIGN AND PLACEMENT ON CAPTURE OF EMERALD ASH BORER, *AGRILUS PLANIPENNIS*

Joseph A. Francese[1], Jason B. Oliver[2], Ivich Fraser[3], Nadeer Youssef[2], David R. Lance[1], Damon J. Crook[1] and Victor C. Mastro[1]

[1]USDA APHIS PPQ Otis Pest Survey Detection and Exclusion Laboratory
Bldg 1398, Otis ANGB, MA 02542

[2]Tennessee State University, Otis L. Floyd Nursery Research Center
472 Cadillac Lane, McMinnville, TN 37110

[3]USDA APHIS PPQ EAB, 5936 Ford Court, Brighton, MI 48116

ABSTRACT

The ongoing objective of this research is to develop a trap that can improve the sensitivity and efficiency of emerald ash borer, *Agrilus planipennis* (Coleoptera: Buprestidae) Fairmaire (EAB) survey and aid the overall program in achieving its goals. As part of this work, we sought to determine the optimal location for trap placement. First we placed purple corrugated plastic panels 15 m inside an ash woodlot, 15 m in an adjacent field and along the edge. We caught more EAB in the field and along the edge than inside the woodlot. In a similar study, we looked at the interaction between trap location and trap color on EAB capture. We placed purple, white and red corrugated plastic box traps inside ash woodlots, in an adjacent field, and along the edge. Purple traps in the field caught more than purple traps inside the woodlot. Purple traps at all locations caught more than white or red traps, and there was no difference in catch between white or red traps.

In addition to optimal trap location, we also evaluated traps of four different designs: 1) a girdled tree with a glue-covered band around it; 2) a purple box trap; 3) a purple crossvane trap with a purple top; and 4) the crossvane with a translucent top. The traps were placed inside a woodlot to accommodate the banded trees. Banded trees caught significantly more EAB than the other three trap types. In a separate study using small nursery green ash we tested four damage types: 1) a crown cut; 2) a root prune; 3) a full girdle; and 4) a trunk scraping. We also tested two controls a rebar pole and an undamaged tree. A purple triangular trap was placed around the base of each tree (and pole). While there were no significant differences between the damage classes and the undamaged tree or among the damage classes, all treatments that included a host were significantly different from the rebar pole control.

From our results we can conclude that purple traps are relatively more effective in open areas than in wooded areas. Banded trees are more effective in wooded areas than other traps tested. We will be performing electroretinographic studies to further evaluate EAB responses to color. It would also be that the beetles are using olfactory cues to aid in finding a suitable host. Currently research is being performed to find potential volatile attractants.

EMERALD ASH BORER DISPERSAL—A RELEASE AND RECAPTURE STUDY

Ivich Fraser[1], Victor C. Mastro[2] and David R. Lance[2]

[1]USDA APHIS PPQ EAB, 5936 Ford Court, Brighton, MI 48116

[2]USDA APHIS PPQ Otis Pest Survey, Detection and Exclusion Lab
Bldg 1398, Otis ANGB, MA 02542

ABSTRACT

This particular study was designed to investigate the emerald ash borer's dispersal behavior. We investigated distance dispersal from a central release point and landing height on trees.

At approximately 15, 30 and 60 meters out from the release location we chose respectively four, eight and 16 ash trees. From each tree a series of metal mesh panels (1 meter by 0.5 meters) covered in tangle foot strung together by 0.5 meter lengths of rope was hung along the length of the tree. The traps were strung vertically parallel to the tree's trunk by climbing a maximum of 10 meters and attaching a pulley to the tree. A rope was then strung through the pulley and the chain of traps was tied to the rope and pulled up along the length of the tree. A rope was tied to the tree holding the last two panels tightly to the tree, in order to keep the panels closely associated with the trunk of the tree.

Beetles used in this study were collected in the laboratory. Heavily infested ash wood was brought into the laboratory and placed in barrels. The adult emerald ash borer emerging from these barrels were collected and marked with day-glow powder. They were then placed in jars with ash leaves and water until their time of release. On the release date the leaves and water were taken out of the jars and the jars were left at the release point to allow the beetles to fly out at will.

Through the summer roughly 6,000 marked beetles were released in this study. Of the beetles released 210 were recaptured. Of the 28 trees, 20 recaptured at least one released beetle; the most a single tree recaptured in total was 29 marked beetles. The tree located farthest out from the release point, at 76 meters, recaptured two beetles. No trends in flight patterns were apparent from recapture rates, they dispersed at random. Furthermore, some trees located more closely to the release point recaptured no beetles, while others further from the release point, along the same direct flight path, did. The trees were either black or green ash and were in various states of decline. A Chi-square analysis of total number of beetles caught in black and green ash was significantly different from random, with more beetles caught on black ash trees. A Chi-square analysis of the total number of beetles caught on trees and the tree's percent relative dieback was also performed. The results were significantly different from random. Trees with 100 percent dieback (dead trees) caught the most beetles. We also analyzed the position of the panels along the length of the trunk and number of beetles detected on each panel using a Chi-square test. The results were significantly different from random. The panels located lowest along the tree trunk caught the fewest beetles and those located highest caught the most beetles. This was a consistent and prominent pattern.

WHAT CAUSES MALE-BIASED SEX RATIOS IN THE GYPSY MOTH PARASITOID *GLYPTAPANTELES FLAVICOXIS*?

R. W. Fuester[1], K. S. Swan[1], P. B. Taylor[1] and G. Ramaseshiah[2]

[1]USDA-ARS, Beneficial Insects Introduction Research
501 South Chapel Street, Newark, DE 19713-3814

[2]377 Main 9, Cross 13, Vyalikaval, Bangalore- 560003 India

ABSTRACT

Glyptapanteles flavicoxis (Marsh) is an oligophagous, gregarious larval parasitoid of the Indian gypsy moth, *Lymantria obfuscata* (Walker), that readily attacks the European gypsy moth, *Lymantria dispar* (L.). This species is believed to have potential for inundative releases against gypsy moth populations, because it can be reared in large numbers with few hosts. Unfortunately, sex ratios in laboratory reared *G. flavicoxis* are usually male-biased. Male-biased sex ratios hinder efforts to mass release parasitic Hymenoptera for biological control by making the production of females costly. Because inbreeding is believed to have adverse effects on the laboratory rearing of natural enemies, we established a new colony of the parasitoid from field-collected material, and maintained it for 16 generations in the laboratory, while comparing sex ratios in progeny of inbred and outcrossed females. Virgin females were allowed to sting hosts prior to mating to insure that only haploid males would be used in the crosses of the next generation. This was done to eliminate any confounding effects caused by the presence of putative diploid males. Only post-mating progeny were used in calculating sex ratios, which were expressed as percent females. Sex ratios of progeny produced by inbred or outcrossed females day were recorded and subjected to two-way analysis of variance using generation and type of cross (inbred or outcrossed) as grouping factors. We used the Holm-Sidak procedure to look for differences in sex ratios among progeny of parents yielding mixed progeny and G-tests to test for differences in proportions of females producing mixed and all male progeny. There were no noteworthy trends in the proportions of females producing mixed progeny over time (generations). Likewise, the proportions of inbred and outcrossed females producing mixed progeny did not differ. When crosses with only male progeny were excluded from the analysis, sex ratios among progeny of inbred and outcrossed females did not differ. Sex ratios appeared to fluctuate more or less randomly over the first 11 generations, but appeared to decline steadily over the last five generations (12-16 inclusive). The study will be continued for several more generations to see if the trend continues.

INTERACTION BETWEEN GYPSY MOTH (*LYMANTRIA DISPAR* L.) AND SOME COMPETITIVE DEFOLIATORS

Milka M. Glavendekić and Ljubodrag S. Mihajlović

University of Belgrade, Faculty of Forestry, Department of Landscape
Architecture and Horticulture,
Kneza Viseslava1, 11030 Belgrade, Serbia and Montenegro

ABSTRACT

Insect defoliators liable to frequent or occasional outbreaks can endanger forestry production and disturb the stability of forest ecosystems. There were studied life cycles, parasitoids, predators and population dynamics of leaf rollers, the winter moths, noctuids and gypsy moth, which occur in oak forests.

Investigations on population dynamics of oak defoliators and complex of their parasitoids were done at the permanent sample plots at the localities in N. P. Fruška Gora, Forest Estate Belgrade and at several localities in Serbia.

During the last 50 years in former Yugoslavia gypsy moth had five outbreaks of acute type: 1945-1950, 1952-1957, 1961-1966, 1995-1998 and 2003-2005. Between 1966 and 1995 there was observed chronic type of outbreak at some localities. There was a marked upswing in abundance but phase of progradation was short and did not cause forest defoliation on large areas. Gypsy moth overpopulated alone.

Investigation on parasitoids and hyperparasitoids (1984-2002) showed that 38 parasitoids and 12 hyperparasitoids were trophically related with nine winter moth species belonging to following genera: *Colotois, Agriopis, Erannis, Alsophila, Operophteri* and *Apocheima* (Glavendekić 2002).

Investigations on natural enemies of leaf rollers (1974-1986) showed that 56 parasitoids and 10 hyperparasitoids were found on altogether 46 leaf rollers which occur in oak forests in Serbia. The most important and abundant were *Tortix viridana* L. and *Aleimma loeflingiana* L. (Mihajlović 1986).

There were found on gypsy moth in former Yugoslavia all together 50 parasitids and 34 hyperparastioids (Ristić et al. 1998). Comparing qualitative composition of parasitoids on gypsy moth, leaf rollers, noctuids and the winter moths it could be concluded that there are few of them related to all hosts (Table 3).

The recent studies indicate that the outbreak of Tortricidae, Noctuidae and Geometridae overlap with gypsy moth outbreaks. Harmful effect on oak trees is prolonged from April when majority of Tortricidae, Noctuidae and Geometridae feed till the end of June when gypsy moth caterpillars complete their development. Due to defoliation and new emergence of leaves, physiological weakening is the most intensive in second half of May till the middle of June. It is common that powdery mildew attack new leaves in June.

THE GYPSY MOTH EVENT MONITOR FOR FVS: A TOOL FOR FOREST AND PEST MANAGERS

Kurt W. Gottschalk[1] and Anthony W. Courter[2]

[1]USDA Forest Service, Northern Research Station,
180 Canfield St., Morgantown, WV 26505

[2]USDA Forest Service, Forest Health Technology Enterprise Team, Ft. Collins, CO

ABSTRACT

The Gypsy Moth Event Monitor is a program that simulates the effects of gypsy moth, *Lymantria dispar* (L.), within the confines of the Forest Vegetation Simulator (FVS). Individual stands are evaluated with a susceptibility index system to determine the vulnerability of the stand to the effects of gypsy moth. A gypsy moth outbreak is scheduled in the FVS multi-year cycle if a drawn random number is less than or equal to the estimated probability of outbreak in that multi-year cycle. If an outbreak is scheduled, gypsy moth mortality is leveled against species deemed susceptible and resistant; basal area growth is increasingly reduced in susceptible species during light, medium and heavy outbreaks, whereas during a heavy outbreak, basal area growth is somewhat reduced in resistant species.

This is a strategic model that demonstrates the potential loss of timber and habitat due to gypsy moth. The user can proactively reduce the stand's susceptibility to gypsy moth and the probability of a gypsy moth event by scheduling appropriate management actions within FVS (see Gottschalk 1993). Due to the limitations in FVS's growth and mortality equations, the variability normally seen in response to gypsy moth defoliation cannot be adequately modeled. As such, the user is cautioned that the best use of this Event Monitor is to show relative differences in responses of stands to gypsy moth rather than predicting absolute responses in individual stands. The Gypsy Moth Event Monitor can be used to prioritize stands for treatment or to estimate the overall impacts to a forested landscape.

The Gypsy Moth Event Monitor is intended for use by those familiar with the proper use and execution of the Forest Vegetation Simulator. It is recommended that the user be well versed in interpretation of standard FVS output. Specific Event Monitor variables can be exported to spread sheet programs for further user analysis.

Literature Cited

Gottschalk, K.W. 1993. **Silvicultural guidelines for forest stands threatened by the gypsy moth.** Gen. Tech. Rep. NE-171. Radnor, PA: U.S. Department of Agriculture, Forest Service, Northeastern Forest Experiment Station. 49 p.

DO BARK BEETLES AND WOOD BORERS INFEST LUMBER FOLLOWING HEAT TREATMENT? THE ROLE OF BARK

Robert A. Haack[1], Toby R. Petrice[1] and Pascal Nzokou[2]

[1]USDA Forest Service, North Central Research Station,
1407 S. Harrison Road, E. Lansing, MI 48823

[2]Department of Forestry, Michigan State University, E. Lansing, MI 48824

ABSTRACT

Wood packing material (WPM) is an important pathway for the movement of bark- and wood-infesting insects (Haack 2006). New international standards for treating WPM, often referred to as "ISPM 15," were adopted in 2002 (FAO 2002). The two approved WPM treatments are heat treatment (56° C core temperature for 30 min) and fumigation with methyl bromide. These treatments aim to kill insects and disease organisms that reside in the wood at the time of treatment. Currently, ISPM 15 allows bark to be present on treated WPM; however, it is not known if insects can infest WPM after treatment, especially when bark is present. In 2005, we investigated whether insects would infest recently milled green lumber that had varying amounts of bark along one edge of each board. This study was conducted as part of an international collaborative effort under the auspices of the "International Forestry Quarantine Research Group" (Http://www.forestry-quarantine.org/).

In June 2005, we prepared over 200 one-meter-long boards from recently cut, uninfested red pine (*Pinus resinosa*) trees. Half the boards were 1 inch thick and half were 4 inches thick. There were four bark treatments: (1) all bark removed; (2) eight small (25 cm²) bark patches retained; (3) two large (100 cm²) bark patches retained; and (4) all bark retained. Half of the boards were heat treated (using ISPM 15 standards) and half served as untreated controls. The boards were placed in a red pine stand in late June and allowed to undergo natural attack for about 3 weeks. The boards were then returned to the laboratory; half were dissected and half were reared.

Overall, bark beetles (Scolytidae), longhorned beetles (Cerambycidae), and weevils (Curculionidae) infested boards in all treatments where bark was retained, including both the heat-treated and control boards. Attacks occurred through the bark. By contrast, these three types of borers did not infest any of the bark-free boards. Based on dissections to date, complete development of bark beetles occurred on boards with all bark retained and with large (100 cm²) bark patches, but not small (25 cm²) bark patches. These results indicate that the presence of bark may pose a risk even when WPM has been properly treated.

Literature Cited

FAO (Food and Agriculture Organization). 2002. **International standards for phytosanitary measures: guidelines for regulating wood packaging material in international trade. Rome, Italy:** Food and Agriculture Organization of the United Nations, Pub. No. 15.

Haack, R.A. 2006. **Exotic bark- and wood boring Coleoptera in the United States: recent establishments and interceptions.** Can. J. For. Res. 36: 269-288.

MICROBIAL CONTROL OF ASIAN LONGHORNED BEETLES—WHAT ARE FUNGAL BANDS?

Ann E. Hajek[1], Thomas Dubois[1], Jennifer Lund[1], Ryan Shanley[1], Leah Bauer[2],
Michael Smith[3], Peng Fan[4], Huang Bo[4], Hu Jiafu[4] and Zengzhi Li[4]

[1]Department of Entomology, Cornell University, Ithaca, NY 148553-2601

[2]USDA, Forest Service, North Central Research Station,
1407 S. Harrison Rd., East Lansing, MI 48823

[3]USDA, Agricultural Research Service, Beneficial Insects Introduction Research Unit,
501 South Chapel Street, Newark, DE 19713

[4]Anhui Agricultural University, Department of Forestry
130 West Changjiang Road, Hefei, 230036 Anhui, China

ABSTRACT

In Japan, the entomopathogenic fungus *Beauveria brongniartii* is grown in nonwoven fiber bands that are placed around trunks of orchard trees for control of numerous cerambycid pests, including *Anoplophora chinensis* (= *A. malasiaca*). The Japanese company producing bands, Nitto Denko in Osaka, markets bands produced from wood pulp. Our program has emphasized developing a method for biological control of Asian longhorned beetle (*Anoplophora glabripennis*) in the United States using similar fungal bands. Highlights in our studies on use of bands containing entomopathogenic fungi for control of adults of Asian longhorned beetle include:

A. Methods for rearing ALB in the quarantine and for differentiating male from female adults.

B. Searching for pathogens in China, finding that entomopathogenic fungi were most common pathogens of *A. glabripennis* in the field. In addition, there were more records of fungal pathogens infecting cerambycids than any other pathogen group.

C. Conducting bioassays with 28 isolates of five species of entomopathogenic fungi (*Beauveria brongniartii*, *Metarhizium anisopliae*, *Paecilomyces farinosus*, *Paecilomyces fumosoroseus* and *Beauveria bassiana*) using larvae and adults.

D. Conducting caged studies with three fungal species in bands in Anhui, China in 2000 and 2001.

E. Conducting noncaged studies with fungal bands in China in 2001, which were repeated with increased replication in 2002.

F. Studying persistence of activity of fungal bands in Queens, NY, using five different fungal isolates from 2001-2004.

G. Presently, studying the effects of fungal infection on fecundity of adult females and contamination of males by inoculated females.

Bands are made using synthetic material that is produced like felt (since it is not woven) but is not compacted, so that ample surface area within the material is available to support fungal growth. We searched for an appropriate substitute for the nonwoven wood pulp material used in Japan because this is not available in the United States and we are using polyester quilt batting for bands. Fungal cells are grown in media on shakers and band material is dipped into mature cultures. Bands are then placed on racks at 100 percent RH for 7-11 days, during which time the fungus grows throughout the bands and produces spores (conidia) on the band surfaces. Bands are placed around tree trunks or branches and adult beetles inoculate themselves when walking. *A. glabripennis* adults are reluctant fliers and frequently walk on tree trunks and branches, especially during the prematurational period when they feed after emergence but before oviposition begins. *A. glabripennis* can become infected after only walking across fungal bands; fungal spores will adhere to the beetle cuticle and entomopathogenic fungi then infect by penetrating through the external cuticle.

SIREX WOODWASP: BIOLOGY, ECOLOGY AND MANAGEMENT

Dennis A. Haugen

USDA Forest Service, Forest Health Protection,
1992 Folwell Ave., St. Paul, MN 55108

ABSTRACT

Sirex woodwasp (*Sirex noctilio* F.) is an aggressive nonnative woodwasp that kills pine trees. In the southern hemisphere, it has caused up to 80 percent mortality in unthinned, overstocked pine plantations. In its native range of Europe, northern Asia, and the northern tip of Africa, sirex attacks mainly pines (e.g., *Pinus sylvestris*, *P. nigra*, *P. pinaster*), but it is rarely a pest (Spradbery and Kirk 1978). In the Southern Hemisphere, it has attacked many of the pines that are native to North America (e.g., *P. radiata*, *P. taeda*, *P. elliottii*, *P. banksiana*, *P. ponderosa*, *P. contorta*).

Sirex is expected to have one generation per year over most of North America, with adult emergence from July through September. Females lay eggs into the wood (up to 400 eggs per female) and also inject a fungus (*Amylostereum areolatum*) and toxic mucus during oviposition. Together, the fungus and mucus kill the tree, and sirex larvae feed on the fungus as they develop. Early symptoms of attacked trees include resin beads or dribbles at the oviposition sites, brown cambial staining, and green needles that reflex. Later symptoms include foliage that turns light green to yellow to red, larval galleries with tightly packed fine frass, and round exit holes that range from 3-11 mm in diameter.

Seven native sirex species occur in North America (*S. areolatus*, *S. behrensii*, *S. cyaneus*, *S. edwardii*, *S. juvencus*, *S. longicauda*, and *S. nigricornis*). However, there are some uncertainties with *S. juvencus* (may be Paleartic in origin) and *S. cyaneus* (may be introduced to Europe). All of these species have conifers as hosts, with varying ranges of pine, spruce, fir, larch, and other conifers (Krombein et al. 1979). However, these North American species use a different species of fungus (*A. chailletii*) than *S. noctilio* (Bedding and Akhurst 1978).

Management of sirex can be accomplished through survey, silviculture, and biological control. Early detection is critical for successful sirex management. The National Strategy for Australia states that sirex should be detected before any compartment reaches 0.1 percent tree mortality (Haugen et al. 1990). Trap trees are a very efficient and effective monitoring tool in the southern hemisphere. Its application in North America will need to be tested due to the native bark beetles and woodborers that may compete for these trap trees. A detection trap may be feasible, but more research in needed on lures (i.e., host volatiles) and trap design. Silvicultural control by on-time thinning will need to be considered in pine plantations and dense fire-regenerated stands.

Another key to sirex management is a parasitic nematode (*Deladenus siricidicola*). It is highly density dependent and specific to woodwasps with the fungus *A. areolatum*. The use of this nematode for sirex control will be presented by Dr. Robin Bedding (See page 21). However, it is important to note that the North American sirex species also have parasitic nematodes (*Deladenus canii, D. nevexii, D. proximus, and D. wilsoni*), and these nematodes require the fungus *A. chailletii*

(Bedding and Akhurst 1978). Also for biological control, parasitoids have been introduced into sirex woodwasp populations in the southern hemisphere, and most are native to North America (e.g., *Megarhyssa nortoni*, *Rhyssa persuasoria*, *Rhyssa hoferi*, *Schlettererius cinctipes*, and *Ibalia leucospoides*), so parasitoid introductions for sirex management should not be needed in North America (Haugen and Hoebeke 2005). For the USDA Forest Service Pest Alert on sirex woodwasp, go to: www.na.fs.fed.us/fhp/sww/

Literature Cited

Bedding, R.A. and R.J. Akhurst. 1978. **Geographical distribution and host preferences of *Deladenus* species (Nematoda: Neotylenchidae) parasitic in siricid woodwasps and associated hymenopterous parasitoids**. Nematologica. 24: 286-94.

Haugen, D.A., R.A. Bedding, M.G. Underdown, F.G. Neumann. **1990. National strategy for control of *Sirex noctilio* in Australia.** Australian Forest Grower. 13(2): special liftout section No. 13. 8 p.

Haugen, D.A. and E.R. Hoebeke. 2005. **Pest Alert: Sirex woodwasp—*Sirex noctilio* F. (Hymenoptera: Siricidae)**. USDA Forest Service, Northeastern Area. NA-PR-07-07.

Krombein, K.V., et al. 1979. **Catalogue of Hymenoptera in America north of Mexico, Vol. 1, (Symphyta and Apocrita)**. Washington, DC, Smithsonian Institution Press.

Spradbery, J.P., A.A. Kirk. 1978. **Aspects of the ecology of siricid woodwasps (Hymenoptera: Siricidae) in Europe, North Africa and Turkey with special reference to the biological control of *Sirex noctilio* F. in Australia.** Bulletin of Entomological Research 68: 341-359.

NEW ASSOCIATIONS BETWEEN THE ASIAN PESTS *ANOPLOPHORA* SPP. AND LOCAL PARASITOIDS, IN ITALY (2005)

Franck Hérard[1], Mariangela Ciampitti[2], Matteo Maspero[3], Christian Cocquempot[4], Gérard Delvare[5], Jaime Lopez[1] and Mario Colombo[6]

[1]European Biological Control Laboratory, USDA-ARS, CS90013 Montferrier-sur-Lez, 34988 Saint-Gély-du-Fesc cedex, France

[2]Regione Lombardia - Servizio Fitosanitario, Milano, Italy

[3]Fondazione Minoprio, Vertemate con Minoprio, Italy

[4]INRA, USC d'écologie animale et de zoologie agricole, Montpellier, France

[5]CIRAD, campus International de Baillarguet-CSIRO, Montferrier-sur-Lez, France

[6]Istituto di Entomologia Agraria, Università degli Studi di Milano, Italy

ABSTRACT

The Asian longhorned beetle (ALB) *Anoplophora glabripennis* (Motschulsky), and the citrus longhorned beetle (CLB) *Anoplophora chinensis* (Forster) (Coleoptera, Cerambycidae) have been accidentally introduced in a few urban sites in North America and Europe where they are considered as serious threats to urban and natural forests, and are subject to eradication. In their native area, both pests cause serious damage to many deciduous trees, mainly in the genera *Populus*, *Acer* and *Salix*. CLB is also a major pest of citrus in Japan. In 2000, the presence of *A. chinensis* was detected at Parabiago, Italy, in the neighborhood of a nursery where bonsais imported from Eastern Asia were grown. Many signs of much older introductions were found since then. A recent monitoring, still in progress, showed that the infested area extends at least 60 km² in the northwest of Milan and affects 16 municipalities. Given the current substantial extent of this infestation, and the density of the established CLB populations, there is a high probability that the status of the pest will be raised soon from "introduced" to "invasive", in Italy. In conjunction with the eradication programs, biological control studies were initiated in order to find, identify, and evaluate the parasitoids that could successfully control the pest.

Parasitization of early stages of both hosts (ALB and CLB) in sentinel plants, placed at three sites within the area infested with CLB in Italy, showed that the egg parasitoid *Aprostocetus anoplophorae* Delvare (very likely originating from the Far East) is specific to CLB. Six early larval ectoparasitoid species, *Spathius erythrocephalus* Wesmael (Hym.: Braconidae), *Eurytoma melanoneura* Walker (Hym.: Eurytomidae), *Calosota vernalis* Curtis (Hym.: Eupelmidae), *Cleonymus brevis* Boucek (Hym.: Pteromalidae, Cleonyminae), *Trigonoderus princeps* (Hym.: Pteromalidae, Pteromalinae), and *Sclerodermus* sp. (Hym.: Bethylidae) were reared from the *Anoplophora* hosts exposed in the sentinel plants. All are known as natural enemies of xylophagous insects in Europe. In this way, six new associations involving CLB were identified, and four of these parasitoid species also accepted ALB as a host. The evaluation of some of these parasitoids is in progress at the European Biological Control Lab, Montpellier, France.

HYBRIDIZATION AND INTROGRESSION OF THE TWO STRAINS OF HOKKAIKDO GYPSY MOTHS AS INVASIONS BY ALIEN SPECIES

Yasutomo Higashiura[1], Michio Ishihara[2], Hirofumi Yamaguchi[1], Nanako Ono[1], Shin-ichi Tokishita[1], Hideo Yamagata[1] and Takema Fukatsu[3]

[1]School of Life Sciences, Tokyo University of Pharmacy and Life Sciences, Hachioji, Tokyo 192-0392, Japan

[2]Biological Laboratory, Hyogo College of Medicine, Nishinomiya, Hyogo 663-8501, Japan

[3]National Institute of Adance Industrial Science and Technology (AIST), Tshukuba, Ibaraki 305-8566, Japan

ABSTRACT

Male-killing refers to the death of male embryos or larvae, and is well known in a variety of organisms, such as plants, mites, and insects (Hurst et al. 1997). We have found male-killing by about 10 percent females in a Bibai, Hokkaido, Japan, population of the gypsy moth, *Lymantria dispar* L., and have found maternal inheritance of the trait (Higashiura et al. 1999). These male-killing females have no cytoplasmic bacterial symbionts, which have been found in many male-killing organisms (Hurst et al. 1997). Male-killing and mitochondrial DNA (mtDNA) are both maternally inherited (Schulenburg et al. 2002). The mtDNA haplotypes of the male-killing gypsy moth in Hokkaido are different from Hokkaido types, and is the same as that distributed widely in Asia (Bogdanowicz et al. 2000), including Tokyo. Goldschmidt obtained all female broods by means of backcrossing, i.e. F_1 females of a cross between Tokyo females (subspecies *japonica*) and Hokkaido males (subspecies *praeterea*) mated with Hokkaido males (Goldschmidt 1930). We got all-female broods by the double check of Goldschmidt's results. Moreover we found that male-killing females in Hokkaido mated with Asian type males produced normal sex ratio broods just as Goldschmidt's theory of sex determination states (Goldschmidt 1934). Therefore all-female broods (or male-killing females) found in Bibai, Hokkaido, are thought as an invasive alien species, because those females have Honshu and Asian types of mtDNA haplotype.

Where do those alien species come from? We studied the genetic distribution of the gypsy moth using mtDNA sequences in Hokkaido, Japan. We found that there were two widely diverse lineages in Hokkaido, or Hokkaido and Asian haplotypes, that have 2 percent differences in each other in mtDNA sequences. The genetic distribution of the two lineages were clearly divided by the Ishikari Lowland (the Lowland between Sapporo and Tomakomai); the Hokkaido haplotypes were in the eastern side and the Honshu and Asian haplotypes were in the western side.

The Ishikari Lowland had been under the sea until 60,000 years ago. There had been no straits between Honshu and the western Hokkaido until 1 million years ago. Hokkaido gypsy moths met

Honshu ones about 20,000 years ago, because the Ishikari Lowland has been found since 20,000 years ago. Since then, the two distinct strains have crossed and introgressed each other.

We studied the genetic distribution of mtDNA haplotypes in the Ishikari Lowland. The two lineages contacted at the Ishikari Lowland. The contact zone was very narrow. All-female broods were only found in the Ishikari Lowland and east of there. They existed at the rate of 10 to 50 percent.

Hokkaido gypsy moth is a subspecies, *Lymantria dispar praeterea* Kardakoff, now. Although there were two distinct genotypes in mtDNA in Hokkaido gypsy moths, we found no morphological differences between the two genotypes in Hokkaido. Honshu males have dark wings, and are somewhat larger than Hokkaido males. The wing color of Hokkaido males was lighter than that of Honshu one. There were some varieties in Hokkaido males. But these variations were not relation to genotypes. These indicate that the gene exchanges have occurred between the two types. But the mtDNA is maternally inherited, and remains in the previous regions.

Throughout the introgression, Honshu morphological gypsy moths were disappeared in Hokkaido. We are investigating what genes and functions were disappeared through the introgression. Hokkaido gypsy moths became a model organism to study the outcome of alien species invading after tens of thousands years.

References

Bogdanowicz, S. M., Schaefer, P. W. & Harrison, R. G. **Mitochondrial DNA variation among worldwide populations of gypsy moths, *Lymantria dispar.*** Mol. Phylogenet. Evol. 15, 487-495 (2000).

Goldschmidt, R. **Untersuchungen über Intersexualität.** V. Z. indukt. Abstl. 56, 257-301 (1930).

Goldschmidt, R. ***Lymantria.*** Bibliogr. Genet. 11, 1-185 (1934).

Higashiura, Y., Ishihara, M. & Schaefer, P. W. **Sex ratio distortion and severe inbreeding depression in the gypsy moth *Lymantria dispar* L. in Hokkaido, Japan.** Heredity 83, 290-297 (1999).

Hurst, G. D. D., Hurst, L. D. & Majerus, M. E. N. **In: Influential Passengers (eds O'Neill, S. L., Hoffmann, A. A. & Werren, J. H.)** 125-154 (Oxford Univ. Press, Oxford, 1997).

Schulenburg, J. H. G. v. d. et al. **History of infection with different male-killing bacteria in the two-spot ladybird beetle *Adalia bipunctata* revealed through mitochondrial DNA sequence analysis.** Genetics 160, 1075 1086 (2002).

ECTOMYCORRHIZAL FUNGI FORMING SYMBIOTIC ASSOCIATION WITH THE AMERICAN CHESTNUT

Shiv Hiremath and Kirsten Lehtoma

USDA Forest Service, Forestry Sciences Laboratory
359 Main Road, Delaware, OH 43015

ABSTRACT

Because of the ever-increasing demand for wood and other forest products and increased restrictive regulations for harvesting trees from public land, commercial farming of forest trees is becoming a necessity. For this, it will be essential to exploit all the available commercial land, whether or not it is ideal for optimal growth of forest tree species. In addition, past use of forest lands for mining and farming have produced vast regions unsuitable for natural reforestation. In southeastern Ohio alone, there are more than 600,000 acres of land that had been subjected to mining, which are now under reclamation program. Nearly 50,000 acres have soil that has a low pH.

Mined land sites are generally known to be nutrient poor and contain soils that are in dire need of stabilization to prevent erosion. Reclamation practices have included use of mycorrhizal inoculum to establish successful plant communities on mined sites. Mycorrhizae benefit the vegetation by increasing a plant's ability to survive in a nutrient poor and water deficient environment. In undisturbed ecosystems, mycorrhizal relationships occur naturally. However, in mined sites these fungi need to be reintroduced into the environment for reforestation to be successful. In addition, newer and improved strains of fungi are required initially to combat and remedy the harmful effects of pollution, before the once indigenous strains can take hold in the affected regions.

We are utilizing American chestnut trees, once common to this region, for reforestation of reclaimed mined sites in southeastern Ohio. We have identified several ectomycorrhizal fungi that can associate with the American chestnut using transmission electron microscope and molecular analyses. We have been planting mycorrhizal chestnut seedlings generated in the laboratory in reclaimed lands to assess the benefits of these fungi on survivability and growth of these seedlings. The studies will benefit both reforestation and reclamation of mined sites as well as restoration of the American chestnut.

BLIGHT-RESISTANT AMERICAN CHESTNUT TREES: SELECTION OF PROGENY FROM A BREEDING PROGRAM

Shiv Hiremath[1], Kirsten Lehtoma[1] and Fred Hebard[2]

[1]USDA Forest Service, Forestry Sciences Laboratory
359 Main Road, Delaware, OH 43015

[2]The American Chestnut Foundation, Meadowview Farms,
14005 Glenbrook Ave., Meadowview, VA 24361

ABSTRACT

Introduction of the fungus *Cryphonectria parasitica* into North America in early 1900s resulted in the demise of the American chestnut, which was once the most dominant forest tree in the eastern United States. While the American chestnut (*Castanea dentate*) is susceptible, its counterpart from Asia, the Chinese chestnut, is resistant to the blight-causing fungus. Researchers attempting to restore the American chestnut have focused both on the eradication of the fungus as well as on breeding blight-resistant chestnut trees. Although crosses between the American and the Chinese yield a blight-resistant progeny, often the hybrids have the characteristics of the Chinese tree, which is a dwarf and lacks the superior timber qualities associated with the American chestnut. Therefore, researchers have been using a "back-crossing" technique where the resistant hybrids are successively backcrossed to the original American tree in order to flood more American genes into the hybrid. By repeated back-crosses, it will be possible to generate a blight-resistant chestnut having all the superior traits of the American chestnut.

The American Chestnut Foundation has developed progeny from the third backcross, which by estimation is 15/16 American. However, traditional techniques of determining resistance (by inoculation of the pathogen and assessment) and growth characteristics (waiting to see morphological traits in the mature tree) have proved to be great hindrances to both the pace as well as the degree of success of the program. Progeny selection procedure can be greatly enhanced by utilizing genetic analysis techniques such as PCR and RAPD analyses. Genetic maps of the American and Chinese chestnut trees have been developed and several markers associated with resistance and other traits have been identified. We are using RAPD-PCR analyses to screen progeny for blight resistance and suitable American traits. This method has the capability of precise identification of true resistant types and potentially suitable progeny for use in restoration. Progeny containing none or only a few of the undesirable Chinese traits (0-2) have been selected from the pool and will be used in further analyses. This technique of screening progeny would be a valuable addition to the breeding program and will greatly contribute to the success of the program.

BIOLOGICAL CONTROL OF MILE-A-MINUTE WEED, *POLYGONUM PERFOLIATUM*: FIRST RELEASE OF THE CHINESE WEEVIL, *RHINONCOMIMUS LATIPES*

Judith Hough-Goldstein

Dept. Entomology & Wildlife Ecology, University of Delaware
531 S. College Ave., Newark, DE 19716-2160

ABSTRACT

Mile-a-minute weed (*Polygonum perfoliatum* L.) is an annual vine indigenous to parts of Asia, introduced into the eastern United States in the 1930s and now established throughout much of the Northeast. Infestations can cause failure of tree regeneration and may reduce native plant species in natural areas. A Chinese weevil, *Rhinoncomimus latipes* Korotyaev, was determined to be host specific to mile-a-minute weed, and a permit for field release was obtained from USDA/APHIS in July of 2004. Mass rearing of this insect is currently under way at the Phillip Alampi Beneficial Insects Laboratory, Trenton, NJ.

Small releases were conducted in Delaware and New Jersey in 2004. Adult feeding damage occurred and weevils survived over the winter, appearing in late April to early May, 2005. In 2005, more than 10,000 weevils total were released at two sites in New Jersey. At a third site, 650 weevils were released on ~30 small plants; all of these plants were killed due to adult feeding. Also in 2005, 400 weevils were released at the Ohio Rivers NWR in West Virginia and 610 at Codorus State Park, PA. A standardized monitoring protocol was used at all sites.

To study the dispersal and life history of the weevil, graduate student Ellen Lake released 450 weevils at each of three sites in Chester County, PA, on 9 June 2005. Weevils reproduced and dispersed up to 200 m at these sites, but most remained within 25 m of the release site. Four complete generations occurred in a cage study conducted at the same time. Adult weevils were present on foliage in the field until vines were killed by frost. Overall, weevil numbers at all three sites increased, with multiple generations apparent throughout the summer and fall. A cage study was also conducted in 2005 to determine the impact of various factors on individual mile-a-minute plants. The addition of 20 weevils per plant on 21 July did not reduce seed production. However, there were dramatic differences in seed production and plant dry weight among plants growing in full sun (average of >2300 seeds per plant), partial sun (670 seeds per plant), or full shade (360 seeds per plant). Thus future studies of weevil impacts must standardize sun exposure.

First release of this insect suggests that it will establish easily, producing multiple generations per year, and that adult feeding on small plants can kill mile-a-minute plants. It remains to be seen whether weevil populations will develop in high enough numbers to significantly impact survival, seed production, and spread of this invasive weed.

REPRODUCTIVE BEHAVIORS OF *ANOPLOPHORA GLABRIPENNIS* (COLEOPTERA: CERAMBYCIDAE) IN THE LABORATORY

Melody A. Keena and Vicente Sánchez

USDA Forest Service, Northeastern Center for Forest
Health Research, 51 Mill Pond Rd., Hamden, CT 06514-1777

ABSTRACT

There is a critical need for information on the reproductive behavior of *Anoplophora glabripennis* (Motschulsky) to provide the biological basis for predicting population dynamics, especially as the population size declines due to eradication efforts. To document the reproductive behaviors (both mating and oviposition) five males each from the Chicago, IL and Queens, NY strains were mated to three virgin females. When each male was approximately 2, 4, and 6 weeks old he was paired with a female of similar age from the same strain (with one exception). To observe reproductive behaviors, a pair was placed together, for 6 hours or less when natural separation occurred, in a 3.8-liter glass jar with an *Acer saccharum* Marshall bolt (3-7 cm diameter and 20 cm long) as a potential oviposition substrate. After mating females were provided fresh *A. saccharum* twigs and bolts weekly until death to assess fecundity and fertility.

The reproductive behaviors of *A. glabripennis* are typical of diurnally active species of the subfamily Lamiinae. When a male contacted a female with his antennae, generally he would quickly attempt to mount and mate. If the female was receptive (did not fight the mounting and allowed access to her genital chamber), he would mate with her immediately after mounting and initiate a prolonged pair-bond. Nonreceptive females would exhibit one or more of the following behaviors: run away, kick with hind legs, hit with antennae, make quick turns, fall or fly. In this case, the male might abandon his attempt and separate or perform a short antennal wagging courtship behavior. Nonreceptive females would generally become receptive after further contacts. Nineteen of the 30 pair-bonds lasted the entire 6 hours and the earliest natural separation of a pair occurred at ~2 hours. During the entire time the male continuously grasped the female with his front or both front and middle tarsi. The natural separations occurred either when a female escaped the male's grasp after displaying antagonistic behaviors (n = 12) or when the male simply walked off the female's back (n = 2). Individual copulation events lasted an average of 2.8 minutes and one to 10 copulations occurred in a bout followed by a male refractory period averaging 95 and 60 minutes, respectively for the New York and Illinois males. During copulations the female held the genital chamber open while stationary, walking or chewing the host for oviposition (the latter more often during later copulation events). Between copulations the female would most often walk or attempt oviposition in the pit she had chewed. The average total time in copula was 34 minutes and this resulted in an average of 56 percent hatch of eggs females laid over their life time. Oviposition (0-5 eggs per female) lasted an average of 12 and 10 minutes, respectively for the New York and Illinois females on these bolts with bark that was only 1-2 mm thick. After a female chewed a pit, she rotated 180 degrees, extended her ovipositor, and used it to find the pit. She then inserted the ovipositor under the bark, used the sclerites at the tip of her abdomen in conjunction with lifting her body (by extending her front and middle legs) several times to pry the bark up, laid an egg, and wiped excretions across the opening using the tip of her abdomen. Females abandoned some pits at various points in the process.

SIREX NOCTILIO, THE NEW YORK STORY

Carolyn Klass and E. Richard Hoebeke

Cornell University, Ithaca, NY 14853

ABSTRACT

Sirex wood wasp, (*Sirex noctilio* Fabricius), was first identified in February 2005 from a Lindgren funnel trap taken September 7, 2004 in Fulton, NY (Oswego County). We followed the development of the events in New York chronologically from this first identification to the results of an expanded trapping program in 2005.

February 22, 2005—Identity confirmed morphologically at USDA SEL.

March 29, 2005—Phase I: Survey of businesses that could have served as a pathway, identifying 5 out of 86 that import products from outside the United States and three that imported from overseas. (Ethan Angell, NYSDAM). Visual survey of wood packing material conducted.

April 13, 2005—USFS aerial survey of 32 mi^2 around Fulton to locate areas for further ground survey. (USFS Kevin Dodds).

May 12, 2005—Phase 2: Ground survey of trees, suspect trees tagged. Trees were felled on May 20, 2005 with landowner permission and logs were collected and sent to APHIS/PPQ Otis laboratory for rearing of adults. Larvae were collected for DNA sequencing also.

June 6, 2005—Molecular analysis tentatively identified larvae as *Sirex noctilio*. (Dr. Nathan Schiff, USFS.) Based on this tentative identification trapping survey shifted from detection survey to deliminating survey.

July-October, 2005—Phase 3: Trapping survey begun with 213 traps, which included 154 Lindgren funnel traps baited with alpha pinene, cis-verbenol, ipsidienol and methyl butenol; 28 Cross Vane sticky traps; and 11 intercept traps baited with alpha-pinene plus beta-pinene, and 20 log traps (no bait). All traps suspended 7 feet above the ground (to bottom of trap).

August 1-7, 2005—Survey expanded and 363 more traps were deployed from a 20-mile radius to a 70-mile radius around Oswego.

Trap results showed *Sirex noctilio* to be present in Oswego County and four other surrounding counties in New York state.

Acknowledgments: NYS Department of Agriculture and Markets, USDA APHIS, USFS and Forestryimages.

HOST RESISTANCE TO EMERALD ASH BORER: DEVELOPMENT OF NOVEL ASH HYBRIDS

Jennifer L. Koch[1], David W. Carey[1] and Richard Larson[2]

[1]USDA Forest Service, Northern Research Station, 359 Main Rd., Delaware, OH 43015

[2]Dawes Arboretum, 7770 Jacksontown Rd., Newark, OH 43056

ABSTRACT

In contrast to the rapid destruction of ash trees in the United States by emerald ash borer (EAB, *Agrilus planipennis* Fairmaire), outbreaks of EAB in Asia appear to be isolated responses to stress, such as drought, and do not devastate the ash population. This indicates that in Asia, ash trees may have a level of inherent resistance. This resistance may be the result of the co-evolution of the Asian ash species with the borer. The hypothesis that native trees may be more resistant to their native pests is upheld by several well documented examples, including a study of birch resistance to the bronze birch borer, a close relative of EAB that is native to North America (Nielsen & Herms, in prep.). In this study, 100 percent mortality was observed in Asian birch species but 75 percent of the birch species native to North America survived. Another example is the high level of resistance that the Asian silver linden has to the feeding of the Japanese beetle (*Popillia japonica*) while basswood native to North America and European lindens are both seriously defoliated by the beetle.

Our goal is to identify Asian ash species that have resistance to EAB and to use them to hybridize with North American ash species to generate novel ash hybrids that retain the EAB-resistant phenotype. A longer-term goal of this research is use backcrossing to generate EAB-resistant ash trees that retain all the characteristics of the native ash species and maintain only the minimum portion of the Asian species required to maintain EAB-resistance. The establishment of such a breeding program will provide the foundation for understanding the mechanism(s) and mode of inheritance of EAB resistance.

A multi-pronged research approach is being taken to generated novel ash hybrids. Efforts at hybridization have focused on crosses between *F. chinensis* and *F. Americana* or *F. pennsylvanica* and between *F. mandshurica* and *F. nigra*. Seed yield has been relatively low. However, pollen germination tests have demonstrated that maximum germination rate is obtained at different pH levels for different *Fraxinus* species, which likely will impact the success of hybridization attempts. Methods to circumvent this problem are being developed. Work is also being done to optimize seed germination for all the *Fraxinus* species of interest. Finally, molecular techniques are being developed to allow hybrids to be distinguished from their parent species.

FIELD TRANSMISSION OF A MICROSPORIDIAN PATHOGEN OF GYPSY MOTH, *LYMANTRIA DISPAR*

Thomas Kolling and Andreas Linde

Univ. of Appl. Sciences, Dept. of Forestry,
Alfred-Moeller-St. 1, 16225 Eberswalde, Germany

ABSTRACT

The quantification of the transmission of entomopathogens is important for the evaluation of their establishment and potential as biological control agents, however, only few field or semi-field studies were performed. The microsporidium *Vairimorpha* sp. was isolated from a gypsy moth (*Lymantria dispar*) population in Bulgaria and is highly pathogenic for gypsy moth. Infective spores are produced in the larval fat body, and to a lesser extent probably in the malpighian tubules and the midgut epithelium. Unlike other microsporidia (e.g. *Nosema* spp. from gypsy moth), which produce spores in silk glands and therefore may be transmitted by contaminated silk and faeces, the exit of spores of *Vairimorpha* sp. from the fat body is still an obstacle. Spores can be released from cadavers of infected larvae or may be ingested through cannibalism. Laboratory studies show low rates of transmission among living larvae.

To study transmission in the field, a study plot was established in the Forest Botanical Garden in Eberswalde, Germany. Cages (1x1x2 m) were built around 10 oak trees (*Quercus petraea*, 3 years old, 2 m height) of similar foliage quantity. *Vairimorpha*-infected (5×10^3 spores per larva) and uninfected *Lymantria dispar* larvae (test larvae) were placed into the cages with a ratio of 10 initially-infected and 90 test larvae, or ratios of 20:80, 30:70, 40:60, 50:50; each treatment was replicated in two cages and repeated twice in the summer of 2005. After 18 days of exposure, all larvae were removed and individually reared in the laboratory for an additional 14 days, then diagnosed for infection using phase contrast microscopy.

The rate of recovery was very high. In total, 87.8 percent of all larvae (72 percent of the initially infected larvae [all alive] and 94.5 percent of test larvae [these either as cadavers or alive]) were recovered after 18 days. Different from previous laboratory experiments, the field experiments revealed a high transmission rate. In particular, transmission ranged from 17 to 67 percent, depending on the ratio of initially infected and test larvae. In some cages we found transmission rates of up to 99 percent. The transmission rates increased with the ratio of initially-infected to test larvae (10:90; 20:80; 30:70; and 40:60), but showed no further increase when the ratio was 50:50.

These unexpected results indicate that the dynamics of the interactions between the insects and the microsporidium *Vairimorpha* sp. in the field seem to be very different from what we find in the laboratory. Remarkably, the correlation between the probability of encounter (of a dead, infected larvae with a test larvae) and the number of infected test larvae is highly significant (rho=0.740**; Spearman correlation coefficient 0.001-level). Based on these results in our field experiments, a significant influence of the presence of dead larvae in the cages on the transmission rates is conjecturable. For 2006 we are planning the next two trials with the same experiment design and hope to broaden the data basis for our results.

MULTIVARIATE STATISTICAL ANALYSIS OF HEMLOCK (*TSUGA*) VOLATILES BY SPME/GC/MS: INSIGHTS INTO THE PHYTOCHEMISTRY OF THE HEMLOCK WOOLLY ADELGID (*ADELGES TSUGAE* ANNAND)

Anthony Lagalante[1], Frank Calvosa[1], Michael Mirzabeigi[1], Vikram Iyengar[1], Michael Montgomery[2] and Kathleen Shields[2]

[1]Villanova University, 800 Lancaster Avenue, Villanova, PA 19085-1699

[2]USDA-USFS, Northeastern Center for Forest Health Research, 51 Mill Pond Rd., Hamden, CT 06514-1777

ABSTRACT

A previously developed single-needle, SPME/GC/MS technique was used to measure the terpenoid content of *T. canadensis* growing in a hemlock forest at Lake Scranton, PA (Lagalante and Montgomery 2003). The volatile terpenoid composition was measured over a 1-year period from June 2003 to May 2004 to follow the annual cycle of foliage development from bud-opening, bud-elongation, bud-maturation, and dormancy to bud-break at the start of the next growing season. In addition to the time dependence of the terpenoid composition, micro-dissections were made in order to analyze separately the terpenoid content of the leaf needle and the leaf cushion. The aim of these analyses was to relate any variation in terpenoid composition to the actual feeding location and period of feeding on the host by the hemlock woolly adelgid. The adelgid technically feeds in the stem wood and the xylem ray parenchyma tissue rather the leaf needle. The time-dependent terpenoid levels indicate that the relative percentage of only three of the 51 terpenoids present significantly vary temporally or spatially. Many of these same terpenoids which vary temporally and spatially on new growth were also identified as potential deterrents/attractants from the principal component analysis of the initial study and they may influence the ability of the adelgid to settle/survive on new growth. Analytical data will be presented that indicates a correlation between temporal and spatial terpenoid levels with the biannual reproductive lifecycle of the adelgid.

Additional, current work has examined the terpenoids present in cultivars of *T. canadensis* to examine if selective breeding of cultivars within the species might potentially possess enhanced natural resistance based on terpenoid profiles. *T. canadensis* cultivars were collected from local arboreta and analysed by the single-needle, SPME/GC/MS method. PCA indicates that the *T. canadensis* cultivars do not possess terpenoid profiles associated with the resistant species from our previous work. Future work will be directed toward assessing specific terpenoids for hemlock woolly adelgid fecundity through infusion techniques.

Literature Cited

Lagalante, A.F.; Montgomery, M.E. 2003 **Analysis of terpenoids from hemlock (*Tsuga*) species by solid-phase microextraction gas chromatography/ion-trap mass spectrometry**. J. Agric. Food Chem. 51(8): 2115-2120.

MEASUREMENT OF IMIDACLOPRID IN XYLEM FLUID FROM EASTERN HEMLOCK (*TSUGA CANADENSIS*) BY DERIVITIZATION/GC/MS AND ELISA

Anthony Lagalante[1], Peter Greenbacker[1], Jonathan Jones[1], Richard Turcotte[2] and Bradley Onken[2]

[1]Villanova University, 800 Lancaster Avenue, Villanova, PA 19085-1699

[2] USDA Forest Service, Forest Health Protection, 180 Canfield St., Morgantown, WV 26505-3180

ABSTRACT

Imidacloprid is a nonvolatile insecticide and its direct quantification is not possible by gas chromatography. In order to ascertain imidacloprid levels in soil and trunk injection treated trees, a sensitive and selective method has been developed using GC/MS to measure the imidacloprid levels in xylem fluid exudates. In May 2005, a stand of hemlock trees in West Virginia were treated by soil injection and trunk injection, while certain trees were selected as untreated controls. Terminal branches from four cardinal points within the crown, mid-crown, and base of the tree were collected and placed in a stainless-steel pressurized cylinder to exude the xylem fluid from the branch cutting. An internal standard, $C^{13}D_3$-imidacloprid, was added to the xylem fluid. Following C_{18}-SPE cleanup of the xylem fluid, imidacloprid and the internal standard are derivatized at the imidazole nitrogen to form the semi-volatile, heptafluorobutyryl derivatives. Derivatized imidacloprid was separated using a splitless injection on a Varian Factor 4 VF-5ms column (30 m × 0.25 mm i.d × 0.25 μm film). The derivatized imidacloprid and internal standard are quantified by mass spectrometry using *m/z* 407 and *m/z* 411, respectively.

A commercially available competitive enzyme-linked immunosorbent assay (ELISA) for imidacloprid provides an attractive alternative to analyzing large numbers of of xylem fluid samples as in the current study. Advantages of the ELISA include its sensitivity (working range of 0.2-6 ppb), simplicity, ease of use, and inexpensive cost; however, disadvantages can arise when structurally simlar, imidacloprid metabolites are detected as false-positives by ELISA. We observed and quantified the cross-reactivities of nine known imidacloprid metabolites. Furthermore, a 1:20 dilution was necessary to eliminate cross-reactivity from the xylem fluid matrix raising the ELISA limit of detection to 4 ppb. Over the course of the next several years, imidacloprid in approximately 4000 xylem fluid samples will be quantified by ELISA with 10 percent of the samples confirmed by GC/MS analysis. Concurrent with the insecticide analysis, population levels of adelgids are being studied with the intent of determining imidacloprid action levels and an insecticide reapplication time period. Results will be presented that address the discrepancy in imidacloprid levels due to the cross-reactivity in ELISA, a comparison of the imidacloprid treatment methods used and the persistence of imidacloprid in treated trees.

OBSERVATIONS ON ADULT *AGRILUS PLANIPENNIS* ON ASH IN MICHIGAN

D. R. Lance[1], I. Fraser[2] and V. C. Mastro[1]

[1]USDA-APHIS-PPQ Otis Pest Survey Detection and Exclusion Laboratory
Bldg 1398, Otis ANGB, MA 02542

[2]USDA-APHIS-PPQ, EAB Program, 5936 Ford Court, Brighton, MI 48116

ABSTRACT

Observations were carried out on adult emerald ash borers, *Agrilus planipennis* Fairmaire, on ash trees, *Fraxinus* spp., in park-like and field-edge settings in South Lyon, MI. Observations consisted of (1) counting beetles in various microhabitats; and (2) tracking behavior of individual beetles for periods of up to 15 min. Observations were made from the ground with the aid of binoculars when needed. Counts of beetles included 158 counts each of beetles per 100 leaflets, beetles seen on bark during 1-min searches, and beetles observed flying in a fixed field of view over 1 min. These counts were made systematically at different levels of the canopy (lower, middle and upper), aspects (north, south), and times of day. In addition, we made 5-min counts of beetles in the understory beneath the study trees.

The vast majority (>95%) of beetles we observed on trees were on the upper surfaces of leaves. The beetles appeared to be distributed relatively uniformly throughout the canopy, but numbers of flights observed were several times higher at the tops of trees than in lower portions of the canopy. Overall, the beetles were active insects and typically used flight to move from leaf to leaf or even among leaflets of an individual leaf. Beetles on leaves spent about three-quarters of their time resting, with most of the remaining time split relatively evenly between feeding and crawling. After one period of several consecutive cool, overcast days, most of the beetles were found on grass or forbs in the understory. On the next sunny day, these beetles returned to the trees at approximately the time when direct sunlight fell on the portion of the understory where they had been resting. Factors influencing this migration to and from the understory are not well understood.

We observed less mating- and oviposition-related behavior than we had perhaps expected. For example, only 4 percent of the beetles we observed during our counts were paired in such a way to suggest that they may have been *in copula*. These observations were made relatively early in the season (mid June), and it's possible that beetles spend higher proportions of their time engaged in reproductive behaviors later in the season. Still, we observed several occasions when one beetle hovered above another for a short period, then landed very near or directly upon the second beetle. For lack of a better explanation, we assume that this is a form of premating behavior even though we never actually observed the initiation of a confirmed mating.

WEATHER, DISTANCE, SYNCHRONY AND MATE-FINDING SUCCESS IN *LYMANTRIA DISPAR*

D. R. Lance[1], A. Liebhold[2] and V. C. Mastro[1]

[1]USDA-APHIS-PPQ Otis Pest Survey Detection and Exclusion Laboratory
Bldg 1398, Otis ANGB, MA 02542

[2]USDA Forest Service, 180 Canfield St., Morgantown, WV 26505

ABSTRACT

Mark-recapture experiments were run from 2002 to 2004 to assess factors that influence capture of male gypsy moths, *Lymantria dispar* (L.), in traps baited with (+)-disparlure. Two plot designs were used. One was a center-release design: six and twelve traps were evenly spaced along two concentric circles with radii of 40 and 80 m, respectively, and moths were released at the center of the circles. The second was a center-trap design: males were released from 12 points around a single trap; i.e., at three distances in each of four cardinal directions. For the center-trap study, several combinations of release-to-trap distances were used (12.5, 25 & 50 m; 50, 100 & 150 m; 50, 150 & 250 m). Laboratory-reared males (NJSS strain) were marked with Day-Glo powder (and, if needed, Sharpie on forewing) and released on the day of emergence. For six replicates of the center-trap plot (all 50, 100 & 150 m), males were released on three consecutive days, but the trap was not put into place until just after the third day's release.

Overall, in the center-trap tests, 6476 males were released and 683 (10.5%) were captured. For the center-release tests, 4781 were released across 34 dates, and a total of 1055 (22.1%) were recovered. In the center-trap study, recapture fell from ≥20 percent or more for males released at ≤50 m from the trap to ca. 5 and 1 percent from distances of 150 & 250 m, respectively. Capture declined from >12 percent of males released on the day the trap was put in place to 8 and <3 percent of males released 1 and 2 days before trap placement. Capture data from the center-release plots was analyzed against a number of weather-related variables. Several measures of temperature were significant when included as a covariate in the model; of those, Growing-Degree Days (base 10° C), when accumulated over days 1 and 2 after the release, provided the best fit (F = 25.95; d.f. = 1, 24; P < 0.001). Recapture was also significantly lower for trials in which rain fell on the day after release (treated as a fixed effect with two levels; i.e., rain or not; F = 7.76; d.f. = 1, 24; P < 0.01). Males tended to be captured in traps that were upwind from the release point; specifically, a regression of displacement of moths in the direction of the wind vs. length of the daily wind vector was significant (r² = 0.27; F = 8.14; d.f. = 1, 22; P = 0.009); crosswind displacement was not significant (P = 0.36). These results should be useful for developing models to: (1) improve estimates of the sensitivity of trapping grids for detecting gypsy moth populations; and (2) assess how mate-finding success might influence the establishment of incipient, isolated populations.

EFFICACY OF BASAL SOIL INJECTION AT DIFFERENT WATER VOLUMES AND LANDSCAPE SETTINGS FOR ASIAN LONGHORN BEETLE CONTROL

Phillip A. Lewis

USDA-APHIS, Otis Plant Protection Laboratory,
Bldg 1398, Otis ANGB, MA 02542-5008

ABSTRACT

The Asian longhorn beetle eradication program currently treats at-risk trees by soil injection with a high volume solution of pesticide placed in concentric rings expanding out from the trunk to the dripline of the tree. Using this method in wooded habitats has previously resulted in no detectable residue in treated trees. Basal soil injection (BSI) uses a high concentrate solution of imidacloprid injected close to the base of a treatment tree. The BSI method was tested on trees in an open environment (park setting and street-side trees) at two water volume rates and on trees growing in a woodland environment (with extensive undergrowth of weeds and ivy and competing roots from neighboring untreated trees).

Methods, Materials & Results

Woodlot. Understory maple trees (2 to 22 inches DBH) growing near large non-host trees (10 to 24 inches DBH) were selected to create intense root competition for the imidacloprid treatment. The maple trees were given one cup of a maximum labeled rate solution per inch of tree diameter, delivered as a basal injection. All applications were made with a modified pump-up sprayer at 30 psi with a 6-inch soil injection probe placed within 6 inches of the base of the tree. After 3 months, maple trees under intense root competition had similar residue levels to trees growing in more open environments. Some of the non-host trees were as close as 6 inches to the small diameter trees, but in fact tree diameter was the only significant factor in differences between residue levels (levels decrease with increasing tree DBH; ANOVA P<0.02).

Street-side Trees. Thirty Norway maple and 30 London plane trees were treated with either ½ cup or 1 cup of a maximum labeled rate of imidacloprid per inch of tree diameter to determine an effective minimum treatment volume. Imidacloprid applied by BSI at the maximum labeled rate in ½ cup of pesticide mix per inch of tree DBH achieved similar residue levels to trees exposed to the more dilute mix.

Sample collection and analysis. Foliage samples were collected for 3 months post-treatment and assessed for residue levels using a commercially available ELISA assay. Composite leaf samples are superior to collections of xylem sap when seeking to determine an average pesticide residue value for a treated tree.

Conclusions

(1) The basal soil injection method can be effectively used to treat trees in woodland habitats where intense root competition from neighboring, non-treated trees is encountered.

(2) An increase in tree diameter results in lower levels of pesticide residue, but all trees were well above the target level of 1.9 ppm (ALB LC50) at 2 and 3 months post-injection.

(3) Reducing the water volume to ½ cup per inch of tree diameter resulted in similar residue values as trees treated with higher volume mixes.

HEMLOCK WOOLLY ADELGID AND ITS NATURAL ENEMIES IN YUNNAN PROVINCE, CHINA: FIRST-YEAR (2005) RESULTS

Li Li[1], Wenhua Lu[2], Michael Montgomery[3], Roy Van Driesche[2] and Scott Salom[4]

[1]Research Institute of Resource Insects, Chinese Academy of Forestry, Kunming, Yunnan, 650244, China

[2]Department of Plant, Soil, and Insect Sciences, University of Massachusetts Fernald Hall, Amherst, MA 01003

[3]USDA Forest Service, 51 Millpond Road, Hamden, CT 06514

[4]Department of Entomology, Virginia Tech University, Blacksburg, VA 24601

ABSTRACT

Chinese and American institutions formed a partnership in 2005 for the purpose of studying and obtaining natural enemies for biological control of *Adelges tsugae* Annand, the hemlock woolly adelgid (HWA), in the eastern United States. We report here the first 6 months (June-November) of studies conducted in Yulong (Lijiang) County in Yunnan Province. Previously, *Scymnus sinuanodulus, S. camptodromus* and *S. yunshanpingensis* had been collected there for shipment to the United States. There are four study sites between altitudes of 2600 and 3200 meters in transitional forest. Besides the hemlocks, *Tsuga dumosa* or *T. forrestii*, spruce, fir, pine, *Keteleeria*, and *Taxus* are present along with hardwoods such as oak, birch and poplar.

Monitoring of HWA life stages began in June, when the progrediens generation was almost completed. Developing sistens generation nymphs were observed in September and oviposition by sistens adults started in November. We measured the percentage of 1-year-old terminal branchlets that were infested and found a greater percentage of infested shoots on the north (16.4%) and south (14.4%) sides of a tree than on the east (6.4%) and west (5.3%) sides, and more infested shoots on the lower (13.2%) than on the upper (8.0%) crown.

Predators were sampled monthly by beating hemlock and pine foliage over an inverted umbrella. The Coccinellidae was the most speciose (34 species) and abundant (51% of specimens) group of the 103 morph species and 703 specimens collected. The most abundant lady beetles in Yunnan were *Scymnus camptodromus* and *S. sinuanodulus*, which were recovered in about equal numbers overall. These two species seem segregated by site characteristics, such as the presence of five-needle pine infested with adelgid, which the latter species frequents more than the former. An anthocorid, *Tetraphleps galchanoides*, was collected in one of the Yunnan sites and exported to the United States.

IS BIOLOGICAL CONTROL A MANAGEMENT OPTION FOR EMERALD ASH BORER IN NORTH AMERICA?

Houping Liu[1] and Leah S. Bauer[1,2]

[1]Department of Entomology, Michigan State University,
East Lansing, MI 48824

[2]USDA Forest Service, North Central Research Station,
1407 S. Harrison Rd., East Lansing, MI 48823

ABSTRACT

We began research on natural enemies of *Agrilus planipennis* Fairmaire (Buprestidae) in Michigan and China soon after its discovery in North America. From 2003-2004 in Michigan, parasitoids and fungal pathogens reduced *A. planipennis* larval populations by ca. 3 percent, and no egg parasitoids were confirmed. During 2005 in China, a gregarious larval endoparasitoid, *Tetrastichus* sp. (Hymenoptera: Eulophidae), and a solitary egg parasitoid, *Oobius agrili* (Hymenoptera: Encyrtidae), reduced *A. planipennis* populations by 56 percent. These results confirm the need for biological control of *A. planipennis* in North America. To that end, we developed methods to rear these parasitoids in our quarantine laboratory in Michigan, and have learned both species have high parasitism and reproductive rates, short generation time, and female-biased sex ratio; additionally, *O. agrili* is parthenogenic. These characteristics are indicators of good biocontrol agents. We are currently performing host range studies for these two parasitoid species, a prerequisite to assess the risk vs. benefit of introducing natural enemies for biocontrol. We also recommend continued foreign exploration for other potential natural enemies, and an expanded search to include insect pathogens of *A. planipennis*.

MANAGING THE EMERALD ASH BORER IN CANADA

Kenneth R. Marchant

Canadian Food Inspection Agency
174 Stone Rd. West. Guelph, Ontario, Canada, N1G 4S9

ABSTRACT

The Emerald ash borer, (EAB, *Agrilus planipennis* Fairmaire) continues to pose a major risk to Canadian urban and rural forests and parklands. EAB now occurs in four counties in southwestern Ontario. An estimated 1 million ash trees in Essex County, Ontario, and millions more in adjacent counties are in peril. Little natural resistance has been observed to this point in Canada.

Canada's official position is that EAB cannot be eradicated. However, the Canadian Food Inspection Agency (CFIA) believes there is merit in slowing the spread of EAB within Canada and protecting the country's vast ash resource. It is assumed that, ultimately, biological control and natural tree resistance will play increasingly important roles in "normalizing" the impact of this very serious pest in North America.

Ash (*Fraxinus* spp.) is a very important genus across much of southern Canada with as many as 3 billion trees across the country at risk from EAB. Ash, in particular the red or green ash (*F. pennsylvanica*) is a major component of most southern and eastern Ontario woodlots and forests and often comprises in excess of 50 percent of these; some woodlots have an ash component in excess of 90 percent. Five species of ash (*Fraxinus* spp.) occurring naturally in eastern and central Canada, and numerous exotic species and cultivars are at risk. Both the blue and pumpkin ashes (*F. quadrangulata* and *profunda* respectively) are considered to be rare or species at risk in Canada and occur naturally only in extreme southwestern Ontario. While the blue ash appears to have some inherent resistance, it too succumbs to high levels of EAB. Pumpkin ash, already decimated as a result of past agricultural activities and urban sprawl in southern Ontario, appears to be extremely susceptible to EAB and may be extirpated from Canada as a direct result of EAB.

Because of the absence of any pheromones or other chemical attractants which can be used as lures in traps and the lag between the initial introduction of EAB into an area and initial detection there, the CFIA relies on risk assessment to prioritize its surveys for EAB. Survey activities are focussed on visual detection around sites to which EAB may have been introduced through human activities in recent years such as RV parks, campgrounds, nurseries, and firewood vendors. Both delimitation and detection surveys are conducted; delimitation to determine the leading edge of EAB in or around an infested area, and detection to ascertain the presence or absence of EAB around high risk sites beyond the known leading edge.

Based on recent research and observations, the CFIA makes two assumptions in designing surveys for EAB:

1. The actual leading edge can be as much as 30 km or more beyond what can be reliably detected through visual surveys and,

2. EAB may be present in an area for as long as 4 years prior to survey crews being able to detect it using visual survey techniques.

Survey initiatives in 2005, concentrated on searching for EAB in high risk areas such as along the Canadian side of the St. Clair River (Lambton County) and at Walpole Island (First Nations Reserve); high populations of EAB had been found along the U.S. side of the river in previous years and the risk of introduction through natural spread across the river was perceived as high. Intensive visual surveys were conducted by the CFIA in all woodlots within 10 km of the river with a 5 km grid system being employed elsewhere in the county as part of the detection survey. Intensive visual surveys were also conducted around known risk-makers throughout southern and eastern Ontario and at high risk sites across the province. In response to a late season discovery of EAB at Brimley State Park in Michigan's upper peninsula, extensive surveys were conducted by Natural Resources Canada-Canadian Forest Service (CFS) along the north shore of the St. Mary's River, and along the north shores of Lakes Superior and Huron; no EAB was detected. Surveys were also conducted in the municipality of Chatham-Kent (C-K) in southwestern Ontario to provide assurance that the outlier in neighbouring Elgin county was not an extension of the C-K population.

Survey activities in 2005 detected EAB along the eastern side of the St. Clair River, (Lambton County, Ontario), adjacent to St. Clair County, Michigan; Walpole Island; and at one site in Elgin County, estimated to be 40 km east of the current eastern leading edge in C-K and almost certainly an outlier population that resulted from an introduction to a rest stop along a freeway (highway 401) an estimated 4-5 years previously.

Canada currently regulates EAB at a county level. Infested counties are regulated by means of either an order signed by the Federal Minister of Agriculture declaring an area as infested, or by quarantine notices issued directly to affected property owners, or both. During 2005, all properties within a 5 km radius of all known infestations in both Elgin and Lambton counties were placed under strict quarantine with only compliant ash and other forest materials being permitted to exit the control zone. This was a new strategy for 2005 and designed to slow the spread of EAB within counties which are not believed to generally infested. Ministerial Orders declaring both Elgin and Lambton Counties as infested, are pending.

Consistent with the position of many of its U.S. partners, the CFIA has shifted its focus from active control programs involving tree removal to enhancement of existing regulatory, communication and research initiatives.

To this point, CFIA policy, on the advice of its science committee, has been to remove all ash trees within 500 m of a known positive in counties which are not considered as generally infested. Consistent with this policy, during the late winter of 2005, the CFIA ordered the removal of an estimated 50,000 ash trees from within the 500 m control zones around the City of Chatham, Ontario, C-K. Recent surveys in the vicinity of the 2005 tree removal sites have detected numerous new finds outside of the original 500-m zones which had been previously surveyed on several occasions and found to be not positive. On the basis of this data, it can be concluded that while tree removal around known positives may reduce some of the immediate risk of population build up and dispersal around these sites, it is not an effective means of eradicating EAB at a site and is not likely to be cost-effective in areas with established, albeit low-level populations. For this reason, the CFIA no longer deems tree removal in areas with any level of established populations to be a viable option and no tree further tree removals are currently planned. Where true outliers are detected and are well beyond what is generally considered to be the leading edge, tree removal may still be considered as a viable option in conjunction with other pest mitigation options, such as pesticides.

The CFIA places high value on regulatory activities to slow the spread of EAB in Canada. Under the authority of the Federal Plant Protection Act and Regulations, CFIA inspectors have the legal right to enter a property at any reasonable time to conduct surveys and to take actions against a pest of quarantine significance. For the most part, compliance on the part of affected property owners has been excellent. For flagrant violations there exists the option to prosecute offenders under the Act. CFIA inspectors also have the right to issue Administrative Monetary Penalties (AMPS) for more minor violations such as moving firewood from quarantines areas. These $400 fines or tickets can be issued on the spot to violators. Twenty-six AMPS were issued in 2005, mostly to persons moving ash firewood from quarantined areas to provincial parks outside of the quarantine area.

There are no immediate plans at this time by the CFIA to use pesticides as part of its EAB mitigation programs; however, it is acknowledged that some pest control products such as Imidacloprid can be highly effective in safeguarding or extending the life of trees in infested urban areas, and the CFIA is supportive of further research in this area and either the emergency registration of these products for use by other federal, provincial or municipal government agencies, or full registration by the manufacturer once all the required data is available.

The CFIA places a high value on communication and consultation. The CFIA sees the campaign against EAB to be a coordinated, concerted effort of all levels of government as well as stakeholders and other partners. For this to succeed, effective communications are paramount. Since the initial discovery of EAB in Ontario in 2002, considerable resources have been allocated to the development of posters and fact sheets, display materials and, in high risk areas public notices via radio and local newspapers. The CFS has, in collaboration with the CFIA and provincial forestry officials developed detailed survey guides for use by inspectors and municipal forestry workers.

As part of its consultation strategy, the CFIA has established advisory committees comprised of researchers, quarantine specialists, operational managers and communications experts from within the CFIA, from other federal and provincial government agencies, and from universities. Canada and the United States have collaborated extensively and openly since the initial discovery of EAB in 2002. In addition to several bilateral committees and panels on which representatives from both countries sit, a Canada/U.S. Operations committee meets quarterly to share information and coordinate strategies vis à vis surveillance, regulatory issues, communications, and pest mitigation.

The CFIA is currently developing a management plan, which will clearly outline its policy for surveillance, control, and declaration of areas as regulated. The emphasis of future EAB initiatives will shift from control and pest mitigation to surveillance, research, enforcement, and communication activities.

RELEASE AND MONITORING OF *LARICOBIUS NIGRINUS* (COLEOPTERA: DERODONTIDAE) FOR CLASSICAL BIOLOGICAL CONTROL OF THE HEMLOCK WOOLLY ADELGID IN THE EASTERN U.S.

David L. Mausel, Scott M. Salom and Loke T. Kok

Virginia Tech, Department of Entomology,
216 A Price Hall MC-0319, Blacksburg, VA 24061

ABSTRACT

Studies are being conducted to determine optimal release procedures for establishment and sampling methodology of *Laricobius nigrinus* Fender (Coleoptera: Derodontidae), a predator of the hemlock woolly adelgid, *Adelges tsugae* Annand (Hemiptera: Adelgidae) on eastern hemlock, *Tsuga canadensis* (L.) Carriere, trees. Three factors examined are: (1) the number of beetles released; (2) location; and (3) time of release. CLIMEX software produced a climate match index of 0.58-0.65 between the original *L. nigrinus* collection area (Victoria, B.C.) and eastern areas infested with HWA indicating adequate climate matching. Laboratry-reared beetles were released at 22 sites from Massachusetts to Georgia and sampling methods for adult and immature stages (i.e. beatsheets and branch clipping) were compared within eastern and King County, WA sites. There were 10 open releases in the 2003-2004 season consisting of the replicated treatments: 300 adults in fall 2003, 300 in spring 2004, or 300 in fall 2003 plus spring 2004 (sum = 600). There were 12 releases in the 2004-2005 season including the new release sizes: 75, 150, or 1,200 adults in fall-spring. In fall 2004, beatsheet sampling recovered four *L. nigrinus* F_1 adults at two of the first 10 release sites. In spring 2005, branch clipping recovered 285 F_2 *Laricobius* larvae from 8 of these 10 sites, however some of these recoveries were *L. rubidus* LeConte. *L. nigrinus* presence was confirmed at 5 of the 10 sites through rearing of larvae to the adult stage. In fall 2005, beatsheet sampling recovered 13 F_2 and 33 F_1 *L. nigrinus* adults at the 2003-2004 and 2004-2005 sites, respectively (4 of 22 sites). To date, *L. nigrinus* has been recovered from Tennessee to Pennsylvania at 8 of 22 sites. The optimal release method is not clear at this early stage of colonization. Branch clipping was significantly better in recovery of *L. nigrinus* and determined presence more frequently than beatsheets in native and introduced habitats.

EMERALD ASH BORER TRAP TREES:
EVALUATION OF STRESS AGENTS AND TRAP HEIGHT

Deborah G. McCullough[1,2], Therese M. Poland[3] and David Cappaert[1]

[1]Dept. of Entomology and [2]Dept. of Forestry,
Michigan State University, East Lansing, MI

[3]North Central Research Station,
USDA Forest Service, East Lansing, MI

ABSTRACT

Emerald ash borer (*Agrilus planipennis* Fairmaire), an Asian buprestid discovered in June 2002, has killed an estimated 15 million ash trees (*Fraxinus* sp.) in southeast Michigan. Larvae feed in serpentine galleries in the phloem, disrupting translocation of water and nutrients. At least 16 *Fraxinus* species in North America are threatened by this exotic pest. Operational programs to contain emerald ash borer (EAB) populations are under way in Michigan, Ohio and Indiana. Quarantine regulations and public awareness campaigns have been implemented to prevent transport of infested ash firewood, trees, or logs.

Effective methods to (A) detect newly established and low-density EAB populations; (B) survey and delimit the extent of infestations; and (C) monitor eradication sites are critical components of the EAB operational programs. Researchers have not yet developed effective lures for adult beetles, which appear to rely on ash volatiles rather than pheromones to locate hosts. Visual surveys for EAB detection that rely on external symptoms such as D-shaped exit holes left by emerging adults are problematic. In recently established or low-density populations, many larvae require 2 years for development and even when exit holes are present, they are likely to be high in the canopy on most trees. Climbing trees or destructive sampling to look for larval galleries is difficult and

expensive, especially on a large scale. Because native *Agrilus* sp. Beetles, including bronze birch borer (*A. anxius*) and two-lined chestnut borer (*A. bilineatus*), are attracted to stressed or declining host trees, we hypothesized that EAB may demonstrate similar preferences.

Our primary objective was to determine whether stressed ash trees are more attractive to EAB than relatively healthy ash trees. In 2003, 2004, and 2005, we compared the number of adult beetles captured on sticky traps and the density of larvae on healthy, stressed and wounded ash. In 2005, we also evaluated effects of tree exposure/ shading and trap height on EAB adult capture rates.

Cut logs and stressed trees—2003 study

In May 2003, we selected 18 similarly-sized ash trees at each of four sites in southeast Michigan (72 trees total). In addition, freshly cut white ash (*F. americana*), black ash (*F. nigra*) and green ash (*F. pennsylvanica*) logs (2 m long x 15 cm diam) from uninfested areas were transported to each site. We established six blocks at each site; each block included a healthy ash, a girdled tree and a tree frilled every 3-6 cm with a hypo-hatchet and Pathfinder herbicide. Three trap logs, one of each species, were placed within the blocks (total of 18 trap logs per site; 72 trap logs total). Trap logs were set vertically and supported by a t-post. A 20-cm-wide band of plastic shrink wrap was wrapped around the trunk of all trap trees and logs, then covered with Tanglefoot. Bands were checked weekly and EAB adults were removed and recorded. Trees were felled in the winter and sections of the trunk and large limbs were debarked to quantify larval density.

In 2003, we found that significantly more EAB adults were captured on girdled trees at all three sites than were captured on the untreated control trees or any of the trap logs. On average across all sites, roughly five times as many beetles were captured on the girdled trees as on the control trees. Trees treated with the hypo-hatchet and herbicide remained generally healthy throughout the summer. They consistently captured more adults than healthy trees or logs but differences between herbicide and control trees were not significant at any site. We found that girdled trees functioned as a sink for EAB oviposition at two sites where EAB densities were low or moderate in 2005. At these sites, larval density differed significantly among treatments and was at least four to five times higher on girdled trees where than on control trees. At two sites where EAB densities were high, nearly all phloem was consumed & larval density did not differ among treatments. Few eggs were laid on cut logs; larval density averaged < 3 larvae per m² regardless of site or log species.

Wounds versus stress—2004 study

In 2004, we determined whether EAB adults were attracted to volatiles emitted from the open wounds associated with girdled ash trees or to volatiles associated with stressed ash trees. We compared adult EAB capture on banded white ash trees in three closed-canopy forests in Washtenaw County. In May 2004, we established six blocks at each site, each consisting of four similarly-sized white ash. Trees within blocks were randomly assigned to one of four treatments: (A) standard horizontal girdling (stress + wound); (B) Garlon 4 herbicide (stress, no wound); (C) vertical wounding (wound, but little stress); or (D) healthy (no stress or wound) (72 trees total). On the wounded trees, we removed an area of bark equal in size to the area removed on the girdled trees. Because most of the phloem remained intact, however, physiological stress was minimal. Adult EAB were collected weekly from sticky bands on the trunk of each tree as before. Trees were felled and sections of the trunk and branches were again debarked in winter to quantify larval density.

In 2004, trees treated with the Garlon 4 herbicide obviously began to decline in June and were dead by mid to late July. Significantly more adult beetles were trapped on the highly stressed Garlon trees than on control trees, but differences in adult capture rates among treatments were not substantial. In late fall when we felled and debarked trees, we found a girdled tree (horizontal girdle) had significantly more EAB larvae than control, wounded or herbicide trees. On average, roughly twice as many larvae were present on the girdled trees as on the control or Garlon trees. Garlon trees, which declined and died by late July, were probably unsuitable hosts by the time most adult beetles were ovipositing. Overall, results indicated that EAB adults were more attracted to volatiles emitted by stressed trees than to volatile compounds associated with wounding.

Comparison of stress agents—2005 study

In 2005, we again compared adult EAB attraction to healthy ash trees and trees treated by either girdling (a physical stress), Garlon 4 herbicide (a chemical stress) or methyl jasmonate (a plant stress-eliciting hormone). Using a completely randomized block design, we established 18 blocks at three sites (total of 72 trees). Trees in nine of the 18 blocks were in open areas; the trees in the other nine blocks were in forested sites. Amount of shading experienced by each tree was qualitatively ranked as 1 (open-grown), 2 (super-dominant extending above the canopy), 3 (shading on one aspect), 4 (edge tree) and 5 (mostly shaded). Sticky bands were placed at 1.5 m on all trees. We placed a second sticky band 3-5 m high and suspended two purple sticky panels (20 x 30 cm in size) in the canopy of half of the trees at each site. Sampling to quantify larval density is in progress.

Overall in 2005, five times more adult EAB were captured on girdled trees than on control trees. Trees treated with Garlon herbicide or exposed to methyl jasmonate captured an intermediate number of beetles and were significantly more attractive to beetles than control trees. Open-grown and super-dominant trees with exposed canopies tended to capture more beetles than trees growing in shaded conditions. Low sticky bands (1.5 m), which are simple to apply and check, captured as many or more EAB as high sticky bands and purple panels throughout the flight season.

Summary and Conclusions

Girdled trees were consistently more attractive to EAB adults than untreated, relatively healthy control trees or cut logs in all 3 years. Until effective lures and traps are developed for EAB, girdled trees remain the most effective means to locate low-density EAB infestations. Results also show that adult EAB respond to volatiles produced by stressed trees, rather than volatiles associated with wounds. Ongoing laboratory studies have similarly shown that the suite of volatiles emitted by stressed ash seedlings differs from the volatiles emitted by healthy seedlings and that EAB adult females are attracted to volatiles from stressed seedlings (see Poland et al., this volume). These results, along with our field studies, indicate that stress-related volatiles should remain the primary focus for lure development. In addition, increased understanding of EAB behavior can likely improve effectiveness of trap trees and eventually EAB lures. For example, sticky bands on open-grown trees or dominant trees were more likely to capture adult EAB than bands on shaded trees in closed-canopy settings. Results from these and related studies indicate that debarking trees to find larval galleries is especially important for EAB detection in low density populations and closed-canopy forests, where fewer adult EAB were likely to be intercepted by sticky bands on tree trunks.

POTENTIAL PRODUCTION OF EMERALD ASH BORER ADULTS: TREE, SITE AND LANDSCAPE-LEVEL APPLICATIONS

Deborah G. McCullough[1,2] and Nathan W. Siegert[1]

[1]Department of Entomology and [2]Department of Forestry,
Michigan State University, East Lansing, MI 48824-1115

ABSTRACT

Emerald ash borer (*Agrilus planipennis* Fairmaire), an Asian phloem-feeding pest discovered in 2002, is established across southeast Michigan and parts of southern Ontario. More than 35 outlier populations have been identified in other areas of Michigan, Ohio and Indiana. An estimated 12 to 15 million ash (*Fraxinus* sp.) trees in urban and forested areas of southeast Michigan have been killed by emerald ash borer (EAB) and all North American ash are threatened by this exotic pest.

Federal and state regulatory agencies launched major programs in 2002 to contain EAB and to minimize economic and ecological damage likely to occur if this invasive pest continues to spread. To date, containment activities at outlier sites involve felling, removal and destruction of all ash trees within a 200 to 800 m radius of trees known to be infested, to ensure that non-symptomatic but infested trees are removed. Limited funding, however, requires officials to prioritize sites and determine how to allocate limited resources most efficiently while achieving a desired reduction in EAB density. Forest managers and property owners must also compare costs and benefits of alternative silvicultural options for stands with a substantial ash component.

Our objectives were to:
1. Develop a model to predict ash phloem area using tree diameter
2. Determine the number of EAB adults likely to emerge from 1 m^2 of ash phloem
3. Apply models to real-life ash tree inventory data to assess effects of alternative tree removal strategies on potential production of EAB.

We measured surface area, as a surrogate for phloem area, on 148 ash trees ranging from 5.2 to 65.0 cm in diameter at breast height (DBH). After felling, trees were sectioned and length and diameter of sections $\geq$ 6 cm diam were measured. Surface area measurements from all sections (estimated as a conical frustum) were summed to estimate the area of phloem available to EAB larvae. A second order polynomial model provided the best fit to the relationship between DBH and tree surface area.

Potential production of adult beetles per m^2 of phloem was estimated by counting distinctive EAB exit holes and woodpecker attacks on 71 ash trees recently killed by EAB. Five to 13 areas (depending on tree size) at 1 to 3 m aboveground were intensively examined on each tree; total area examined ranged from 0.17 to 3.73 m^2 per tree. Number of *A. planipennis* produced per tree ranged from 17 to 170 per m² of phloem, but mean and median values consistently hovered around 100 beetles per m². Beetle production was roughly 20 percent lower in small trees than in trees that were ≥ 14 cm (4 inches) in diameter. When the smallest trees (< 14 cm DBH) were excluded, an average of 110.3 ± 6.25 beetles developed per m² of phloem.

We estimated available phloem and potential EAB production by diameter class for trees at an outlier site in southwest Michigan in the town of St. Joseph. To eradicate this population, regulatory officials delineated an area with a radius slightly greater than 800 m for ash tree removal. Using a 100 x 100 m grid overlaid on the affected area, survey crews measured and marked all ash trees, then tallied the trees by diameter class in each grid cell. Contractors felled, removed and destroyed more than 21,000 ash trees from the site in April 2004. We applied our models to the St. Joseph ash inventory data to estimate potential EAB production by size class at a 200 to 800 m radius around the epicenter of the infestation.

In the treated area (800 m radius), nearly 80 percent of the 21,429 ash trees were small (< 14 cm or 5 inches DBH). Despite their abundance, small trees accounted for less than 10 percent of the total number of EAB that could have been produced in the area. In contrast, trees with commercial value (> 26 cm or 10 inches DBH) comprised only 6.3 percent of the 21,429 trees in the treated area, but would have produced almost 70 percent of the beetles. The St. Joseph site also illustrates the importance of ash tree distribution. Removing ash trees within the first 200 m of the infestation epicenter (an area of 0.13 km²), a highly urban area, would have reduced EAB production by less than 2 percent. In contrast, many large ash trees in the forested and riparian areas that were 600 to 800 m from the epicenter (still a 0.13 km² area) would have produced 58 percent of the beetles.

Results show that effectiveness of EAB containment options, such as removing trees within varying areas or removing only large trees, will be determined by the abundance, size and spatial distribution of ash trees in relation to the source or epicenter of an outlier infestation. More broadly, our models estimate potential EAB production for individual ash trees or for any area of interest where the abundance and size of ash trees is known. This information should help regulatory officials and foresters more accurately evaluate costs and benefits of EAB management options.

HEIGHT PREFERENCE OF *SCOLYTUS SCHEVYREWI* SEMENOV, THE BANDED ELM BARK BEETLE OF AMERICAN ELM, *ULMUS AMERICANA*

S. McElwey[1], J. F. Negrón[2], and J. Withrow[3]

[1]Department of Bioagricultural Sciences and Pest Management, Colorado State University, Fort Collins, CO 80523

[2]USDA Forest Service, Rocky Mountain Research Station, 240 W. Prospect, Fort Collins, CO 80525

[3]SI International, Inc., 2629 Redwing Road, Suite 110, Fort Collins, CO 80526

ABSTRACT

Scolytus schevyrewi Semenov, the banded elm bark beetle, was first detected in North America in April 2003 in Colorado and Utah by the Rapid Detection and Response Pilot Project sponsored by APHIS and USDA Forest Service, Forest Health Protection. It was captured in Lindgren funnel traps baited with *a-pinene*, ethanol, and the *Ips typographus* pheromone. After its detection, studies were initiated in June 2003 and are continuing on its biology and chemical ecology. Since April 2003, *S. schevyrewi* has been detected in 21 states. Current literature and research indicates that *S. schevyrewi* seems to be behaving much like *Scolytus multistriatus* Marsham, the smaller European elm bark beetle (Negrón et al. 2005).

S. schevyrewi is known to have a high reproductive potential. The female oviposits an average of 60 (ranging from 23 to 123) eggs per gallery (Li et al. 1987, Wang 1992). In addition, literature from research conducted in China states that the sex ratio is slightly female biased (females: males = 1.0:0.9). More females could give *S. schevyrewi* a competitive advantage over other species such as *S. multistriatus* that occupy the same ecological niche. However, studies conducted in the United States have observed an even 1:1 female:male ratio (Negrón et al. 2005). With a higher reproductive potential and an earlier emergence in the spring, *S. schevyrewi* has the potential to displace of *S. multistriatus* (McElwey, unpublished data). This study evaluated the preferred attack site on American elm of *S. schevrewi* and *S. multistriatus*. Trap height influenced beetle catches. Significantly more beetles were observed on sticky traps located at 5 and 8 ft above ground than traps located higher in the tree. For the statistical comparisons, pairwise comparisons were performed across treatment means of log-transformed data using Tukey adjustment. Overall, more *S. schevyrewi* were collected on the traps than *S. multistriatus*. An increased number of *S. schevyrewi* were collected on the traps situated 5 to 6 ft above the ground. Significantly more *S. shevyrewi* than *S. multistriatus* were collected on all of the other traps. Both *S. schevyrewi* and *S. multistriatus* prefer the same site for colonization of American elm.

FIELD CAGE EVALUATIONS OF THE LADY BEETLE *SCYMNUS SINUANODULUS* FOR BIOLOGICAL CONTROL OF THE HEMLOCK WOOLLY ADELGID

Michael Montgomery[1], Carole A. S-J. Cheah[2] and Christopher Asaro[3]

[1]USDA Forest Service, Northeastern Center for Forest Health Research, Hamden, CT
[2]Connecticut Agricultural Experiment Station, Windsor, CT
[3]University of Georgia, Department of Entomology, Athens, GA

ABSTRACT

Biological control has been a major focus of efforts to reduce the impact of hemlock woolly adelgid (HWA) on hemlocks in the eastern United States. The lady beetle *Scymnus sinuanodulus* Yu et Yao, one of the most abundant predators of HWA in China, was first imported in 1996. Subsequently its biology and host range were evaluated in quarantine and limited numbers are now available for field release.

In 2005, cage field trials were conducted at Coweeta Hydrological Laboratory, Otto, NC, and at Saugatuck Reservoir, Easton, CT, to evaluate reproduction of the lady beetles under field conditions. Fabric bags, each containing three females and two males, were placed over approximately 0.5 m of the terminal end of hemlock branches on March 18, 2005 (North Carolina) and April 22, 2005 (Connecticut). The female lady beetles were laying eggs in the laboratory prior to placement in the field. The bagged hemlock terminals, with the HWA and beetles in them, were removed June 8, 2005 (North Carolina) and June 13 (Connecticut).

The lady beetle reproduced in each of the 20 bags at North Carolina, with a range of 9 to 82 progeny in each bag. Initially, each bag contained more than 100 HWA adult sistentes; at the end of the trial, 0 to 177 progredientes remained in each bag. The number of beetle progeny in the bags was positively correlated with the number of HWA present in the bag at the end of the trial. Most of the progeny recovered were adults.

Similar results were observed in Connecticut, except that initial HWA populations were lower. Only one bag had adelgid ovisacs at the end of the test and this bag had the highest number of progeny (68). All progeny recovered in Connecticut were in the larval stage, except for three prepupae.

The trials in both states indicate that *S. sinuanodulus* reproduces well in the field when prey is not limiting and can dramatically reduce HWA populations.

ENHANCEMENT OF FOREIGN COLLECTION AND QUARANTINE EVALUATION OF HEMLOCK WOOLLY ADELGID NATURAL ENEMIES

Mike Montgomery[1], Roy Van Driesche[2], Scott Salom[3], Wenhua Lu[2], Guoyue Yu[4], Jianhua Zhou[5], Li Li[6] and Shigehiko Shiyake[7]

[1]USDA Forest Service, Northeast Research Station, Hamden, CT 06514

[2]Entomology/PSIS, University of Massachusetts, Amherst, MA, 01003

[3]Department of Entomology, Virginia Tech, Blacksburg, VA , 24601

[4]Beijing Academy of Agricultural and Forestry Sciences, Institute of Plant and Environmental Protection, Beijing, 100081, China

[5]Institute of Forest Protection, Sichuan Academy of Forestry, Chengdu, 610066, China

[6]Research Institute of Resource Insects, Chinese Academy of Forestry, Kunming, Yunnan, 650244, China

[7]Osaka Museum of Natural History, Nagai Park, Osaka, Japan

ABSTRACT

The objectives of this newly funded Forest Service activity are to promote the biological control of hemlock woolly adelgid (*Adelges tsugae* Annand) by (1) hiring an entomologist to work in Asia; (2) revisit known collecting sites and find promising new ones; (3) study the life history and phenology of HWA and its predators; (4) establish protocols for estimating the host ranges of candidate biological agents for use against HWA; (5) enhance quarantine facility capacity; and (6) ship more natural enemies (more species, more individuals) to U.S. quarantine. Initial work is focused in central China (Shaanxi, Sichuan and Yunnan Provinces) and central Japan. An entomologist trained in America, Wenhua Lu, has been contracted to work overseas in China. Additionally, agreements have been made with experts in each country to conduct and assist with field research in China and in Japan. This project builds on previous collecting and study of HWA natural enemies by Mike Montgomery, Scott Salom, and previous cooperators in China.

Work in China has been initiated at eight sites (three in Sichuan, four in Yunnan, and one in Shaanxi). Sites are mostly remote, mountainous slopes with small hemlock stands. Collecting and research teams were formed through cooperative agreements with provincial institutions and training provided to team members on collection and recognition of HWA lifestages and its natural enemies as needed. The study of HWA phenology in China suggests that it differs from that in the eastern United States and that there may be a third generation, as eggs are present in August and September, which is usually not the case in the eastern United States. HWA density (as percentage of branch tips with HWA) ranged from 6 to 11 percent. Predator complexes were examined by beat sheet sampling at the principal study sites. The Coccinellidae (lady beetles) is the predator group that has the greatest diversity and has the must abundant species. *Laricobius* beetles and anthrocorid bugs also play an important role in regulating HWA in China. In Sichuan Province the dominant coccinellid predators were *Scymnus camptodromus*, *S. geminus* and *S. lycotropus*. In Yunnan Province, the dominant species were *S. camptodromus* and *S. sinuanodulus*. Collecting from pine vs hemlock revealed high fidelity of *S. camptodromus* to hemlock, *S. geminus* to pine, and an even split between pine and hemlock for *S. lycotropus* and *S. sinuanodulus*. A few *Laricobius* spp. also were collected. In 2006 an intense effort at optimal times will be made to import the *Laricobius* species and *S. lycotropus*.

In Japan, Mr. Shiyake has established a study site where HWA has the same genetics as in the eastern United States and *Sasjiscymnus tsugae* was collected previously for export to the United States. He has discovered a new species of *Laricobius* at this site, which will be exported to the United States in early 2006. Exploration for natural enemies in other areas of Japan will begin in 2006.

PATHOGENICITY OF TWO NUCLEOPOLYHEDROVIRUS PRODUCTS, VIRIN NSh AND GYPCHEK, FOR ASIAN AND NORTH AMERICAN GYPSY MOTH LARVAE

John Podgwaite[1], Viatcheslav Martemyanov[2] and Stanislav Bakhvalov[2]

[1]USDA Forest Service, Northeastern Center for Forest Health Research,
51 Mill Pond Rd., Hamden, CT 06514-1777

[2]Institute of Systematics and Ecology of Animals SB of RAS,
Novosibirsk, Russia

ABSTRACT

Periodic intrusions of Asian strains of gypsy moth, *Lymantria dispar* L., into North America have occurred over the past several years. Preventative measures in the countries of origin and around ports of entry in North America have lowered the risk of invasion and establishment but the threat remains current. Asian strains have a wider host range than the established North American (European) strain and, unlike North American female moths, Asian females fly. Thus, if an Asian strain were to become established in North America its management would be costly and the potential for damage to forested ecosystems would be great. The gypsy moth nucleopolyhedrovirus (LdNPV) product Gypchek is the only gypsy moth-specific pesticide available for mitigating damage caused by moderate to dense larval populations of the pest. A similar product, Virin NSh, is available in Russia. In the United States Gypchek would be the pesticide of choice for use on environmentally sensitive lands infested by an Asian strain: broad-spectrum pesticide treatments on such lands would be inappropriate. The effective use of Gypchek against these infestations will come through an understanding of LdNPV epizootiology in Asian strain habitats, and, the establishment of Gypchek field doses for use against these strains. As an initial step in establishing field doses we conducted bioassays of both Gypchek and Virin NSh against North American (New Jersey-laboratory) and Asian (Western Siberian-wild) second instar gypsy moth larvae. Diet incorporation assays of both products were conducted in Hamden and birch-foliage assays were conducted in Novosibirsk. Probit analysis of the diet incorporation assay indicated that Gypchek [LC_{50} = 2.52 x 10^4 viral occlusion bodies (OBs)/ml diet] was slightly more active than Virin NSh [LC_{50} = 5.16 x 10^4 OBs/ml diet]. However, parallel regression lines and overlapping of 95 percent confidence limits indicated that the two products were of similar potency. In the assay on birch foliage, larvae were almost identical in their response to the two products, though higher levels of virus were required to elicit an LC_{50}: Gypchek = 1.31 x 10^6 OBs/0.25 m^2 foliage and Virin NSh = 1.20 x 10^6 OBs/0.25 m^2. The slopes of the regressions were nearly identical and were parallel. Comparisons of the results of the two bioassays, though tempting, may be misleading owing to differences in assay protocols. Nevertheless, it is highly probable that both products contain the same virus and will be equally effective when tested against a given strain of gypsy moth. Whether of not Asian strains of gypsy moth are more or less susceptible to Gypchek will be the focus of future studies.

ADAPTATION DURING NORTHERN RANGE EXPANSION IN THE ELONGATE HEMLOCK SCALE *FIORINIA EXTERNA*

Evan Preisser[1], Alexandra Lodge[2], David Orwig[3] and Joseph Elkinton[1]

[1]University of Massachusetts at Amherst, Amherst, MA

[2]Kenyon College, Gambier, OH

[3]Harvard Forest, Petersham, MA

ABSTRACT

The elongate hemlock scale *Fiorinia externa*, (EHS) an invasive pest from Japan, was first found in the eastern United States in 1908. It feeds on a variety of plants, most notably the eastern hemlock *Tsuga canadensis*, and has been spreading slowly into southern New England. In order to examine the northern spread of EHS and the possibility of local adaptation in this insect, we first performed a field survey in which we resurveyed 141 hemlock stands (first surveyed in 1997-98; see Orwig et al. 2002 for details) in a 7500 km² transect from southern Connecticut to northern Massachusetts. In each stand, we measured adelgid and EHS abundance for 50 trees on a 0-3 scale (0=no EHS, 1=1-10 EHS/m branch, 2=10-100 m/branch, 3=>100/m branch). We also assessed overall hemlock canopy vigor in each stand. We found that EHS continues spreading north and east into New England, and has sharply increased in both density and abundance between 1997-98 and 2005. When latitude and hemlock woolly adelgid density are taken into account, however, EHS density did not correlate with hemlock canopy vigor at the stand level. In a separate experiment designed to assess whether northern populations of EHS show greater cold tolerance than do southern populations, we collected EHS-infested hemlock foliage from four Maryland sites (southern population) and four Connecticut sites (northern population) in March 2004. We then used a freezer to expose EHS-infested foliage to one of seven treatments: 0, 6, 12, 18, 24, 30, or 36 hours at -15°C. One week after the treatments were applied, we counted the percent of surviving scales (up to 100 scales/branch) per treatment per site per location (MD or CT). In the absence of cold shock, southern EHS populations had higher survival than did northern populations. Survival of southern EHS decreased significantly as the length of the cold shock treatment increased; in contrast, survival of northern EHS populations was unaffected by up to 36 hours at -15°C. Our finding that northern EHS populations are more cold-tolerant than southern populations suggests that local adaptation has facilitated this species' invasion.

THE ASSOCIATION OF *XYLEBORUS GLABRATUS* AND AN *OPHIOSTOMA* SPECIES WITH MORTALITY OF RED BAY AND SASSAFRAS IN THE SOUTHEASTERN U.S.

Robert J. Rabaglia[1] and Stephen Fraedrich[2]

[1]USDA Forest Service, Forest Health Protection1601 N. Kent St, RPC7, Arlington, VA 22209

[2]USDA Forest Service, Southern Research Station, 320 Green St., Athens, GA 30602

ABSTRACT

Extensive mortality of red bay (*Persea borbonia* [L.] Spreng) has been reported in coastal areas around Hilton Head Island, SC, and Savannah, GA, since the fall of 2003. In November, 2004 dead and dying red bay trees were examined on Hilton Head Island. Trees exhibited wilt-like symptoms and a distinct discoloration of the sapwood. Leaves on affected trees developed reddish to purplish brown discoloration and were persistent on branches. Samples from dead and dying red bay were collected and found to be infested with *Ambrosiodmus obliquus* (LeConte), *Xyleborinus gracilis* (Eichhoff) and numerous *X. glabratus* (Eichhoff). Samples of symptomatic tissues were also plated on various agar media and an anamorphic fungus was consistently isolated. This fungus has been subsequently identified as an *Ophiostoma* sp. (T. Harrington, personal communication), and morphological and molecular characterizations of the fungus are being conducted. Field and growth chamber studies have subsequently determined that the fungus is pathogenic to red bay and is capable of causing wilt in inoculated plants.

As of February of 2006, surveys have confirmed the presence of the disease in 10 coastal counties of South Carolina and Georgia. In the spring of 2005 the disease was also discovered near Jacksonville, FL. Most red bay trees are now dead in those areas where the disease has been observed since 2003. In all locations where the wilt has been observed, trees were infested by *X. glabratus*, and the *Ophiostoma* sp. was isolated from symptomatic plant tissues. Mortality of sassafras (*Sassafras albidum* (Nutt.) Nees) has also been found in some Georgia counties affected by the wilt of red bay. The dead and dying sassafras exhibit wilt-like symptoms and sapwood discoloration similar to that found in red bay. Laboratory analyses have found that the affected sassafras were also infested with *X. glabratus*, and the *Ophiostoma* sp. was also isolated from symptomatic sapwood.

Xyleborus glabratus was first detected in the United States in 2002 near Port Wentworth, GA. The beetles were collected in traps that were part of a pilot project for the early detection of bark beetles at ports of entry. This project is being conducted by the USDA Forest Service in cooperation with APHIS, state agencies and universities. The subsequent discovery that *X. glabratus* was associated with dead and dying red bay on Hilton Head Island in November of 2004 was the first indication that this beetle was established in forests within the United States. *Xyleborus glabratus* is native to southern and eastern Asia, and its hosts in Asia are primarily in the Lauraceae. In North America its two recorded hosts, red bay and sassafras, are also members of this family. The beetle is a small, but distinctive member of the ambrosia beetle tribe xyleborini. There are 40 members of this tribe in North America, 19 of which are non-native. Many of these non-native species are from southeastern Asia, and have been introduced within the past 20 years. Although only a few of these species have become pests, some species occasionally cause losses of apparently healthy or slightly weakened landscape trees and nursery stock.

All species in the xyleborini are ambrosia beetles that carry symbiotic fungi. Adult females vector spores of the fungi which grow in the galleries in the infested tree. Entrance holes and galleries of *X. glabratus* in red bay were found to have staining and signs of fungal infection. Studies are continuing to better understand the relationship between *X. glabratus* and the *Ophiostoma* sp., as well as better understand the epidemiology of this disease.

DENSITY-DEPENDENT RESISTANCE OF THE GYPSY MOTH, *LYMANTRIA DISPAR*, TO ITS NUCLEOPOLYHEDROVIRUS

James R. Reilly and Ann E. Hajek

Department of Entomology, Cornell University, Ithaca, NY

ABSTRACT

The processes controlling disease resistance can strongly influence the population dynamics of insect outbreaks. Evidence that disease resistance is density-dependent is accumulating, but the exact form of this relationship is highly variable from species to species. It has been hypothesized that insects experiencing high population densities might allocate more energy to disease resistance than those at lower densities, because they are more likely to encounter density-dependent pathogens. In contrast, the increased stress of high-density conditions might leave insects more vulnerable to disease. Both scenarios have been reported for various outbreak lepidoptera in the literature. We tested the relationship between larval density and disease resistance with the gypsy moth (*Lymantria dispar*) and a nucleopolyhedrovirus (LdNPV), one of its most important density-dependent mortality factors, in a series of bioassays. In this system, resistance to the virus decreased with increasing larval density. Similarly, time to death was faster at high densities than at lower densities. Implications of this relationship for insect-pathogen population dynamics were explored.

EMERALD ASH BORER RESPONSES TO INDUCED PLANT VOLATILES

Cesar Rodriguez-Saona[1,2], Therese M. Poland[3], James Miller[1], Lukasz Stelinski[1], Linda Buchan[4], Gary Grant[4], Peter de Groot[4] and Linda MacDonald[4]

[1]Department of Entomology, Michigan State University, E. Lansing, MI 48824

[2]Current address: Blueberry and Cranberry Research Center, Rutgers University, 125A Lake Oswego Rd., Chatsworth, NJ 08019

[3]USDA Forest Service, North Central Research Station, 1407 S. Harrison Rd., Rm. 220,E. Lansing, MI 48823

[4]Canadian Forest Service, Great Lakes Forestry Centre, 1219 Queen St. E., Sault Ste. Marie, Ontario, Canada P6A 5M7

ABSTRACT

Herbivore feeding and methyl jasmonate, a volatile derivative of the stress-eliciting plant hormone, jasmonic acid, induce responses in plants which include the synthesis and emission of volatiles. These induced volatiles can serve to attract or repel herbivores; therefore, they may have potential use in pest management programs. The exotic emerald ash borer (EAB), *Agrilus planipennis* Fairmaire (Coleoptera: Buprestidae), has killed an estimated 15 million ash trees in southeastern Michigan and Windsor, Ontario, since its discovery in 2002. Accurate delimitation of the infested area and detection of new outlier infestations is critical for regulatory officials who must establish quarantine boundaries and implement eradication and control measures. Trapping and detection techniques would greatly enhance efforts to delineate the distribution of the emerald ash borer and locate new infestations.

We tested emerald ash borer responses to ash volatiles produced by adult feeding or treatment with methyl jasmonate. Volatiles from Manchurian ash, *Fraxinus mandshurica*, a species from the emerald ash borer's native range, were tested in a two-choice walking olfactometer bioassay. Male and female adults were given a choice between clean air and 1) seedlings damaged by feeding of 15-20 emerald ash borer adults for 7 days (15-20% leaf area removed); 2) seedlings treated overnight with 1.4 mM methyl jasmonate solution; 3) healthy unmanipulated ash seedlings; and 4) clean air. Female emerald ash borers were attracted to ash seedlings with feeding damage and those that had been treated with methyl jasmonate, but not to healthy ash seedlings or clean air.

Ash volatiles were collected from seedlings damaged by emerald ash borer feeding, seedlings treated with methyl jasmonate, and unmanipulated controls. Both feeding damage by adult emerald ash borers and methyl jasmonate treatment increased volatile emissions from ash compared to controls. Aeration extracts were analyzed by coupled gas chromatographic electro-antennographic detection (GC-EAD) to identify induced compounds from Manchurian ash that elicited an electrophysiological response from the antennae of adult emerald ash borers. At least 10 compounds from ash were found to be antennally active: hexanal, (E)-2-hexenal, (Z)-3-hexen-1-ol, 3-methyl butylaldoxime, (Z)-3-hexen-1-yl acetate, hexyl acetate, (E)-ß-ocimene, linalool, 4,8-dimethyl-1,3,7-nonatriene, and E,E-ȧ-farnesene. Further studies are planned to determine emerald ash borer responses to combinations of the antennally-active compounds in the laboratory and in field trapping experiments. Ultimately, the results may lead to the development of an improved monitoring and detection system for emerald ash borer.

ESTABLISHMENT OF *LARICOBIUS NIGRINUS* (COLEOPTERA: DERODONTIDAE) FOR BIOLOGICAL CONTROL OF HEMLOCK WOOLLY ADELGID

Scott M. Salom, Loke T. Kok, David L. Mausel, Theresa A. Dellinger, Brian M. Eisenback and Robbie W. Flowers

Department of Entomology, Virginia Tech
Blacksburg, VA 24061

ABSTRACT

Laricobius nigrinus is a natural predator of hemlock woolly adelgid (HWA), native to the western hemlock forests of North America. Research over the past 8 years at Virginia Tech has shown that this prey-specific predator is highly adapted to HWA. Several ongoing studies were reported on and will briefly be mentioned here.

Mass rearing efforts are ongoing at three labs in the southern United States. The objective is to produce as many adult beetles as possible for open release. The 2005 Virginia Tech *L. nigrinus* colony was founded with 713 wild-caught adults from Washington. Larval production was good, with 19,593 mature larvae produced. However, we had significant problems with water saturation and mold growth (*Penicillium* sp.) in the aestivation medium over the summer, resulting in high larval/pupal mortality (82.5%), with only 3,424 adults emerging. We will use a smaller aestivation container with improved ventilation to avoid this problem in 2006.

Between fall 2003 and fall 2005, nearly 12,000 beetles have been released at over 30 separate sites in the eastern U.S. Mausel et al. (this publication) reports on beetle recoveries post-release, and it appears that the insects are surviving and are becoming established at several releases sites. As part of this effort, we are attempting to document all releases of *L. nigrinus* in a database, including past and current releases of insectary-reared beetles and direct releases of field-caught beetles. Releases are being made using a newly revised protocol. Pre- and post-release data will be used evaluate the release protocol and document the overall success of the *L. nigrinus* release program. All release cooperators have agreed to collect and send these data to Virginia Tech for summarizing.

We have been looking at the potential interactions between two prey-specific predators, *L. nigrinus* and *Sasajiscymnus tsugae*, with a generalist established predator, *Harmonia axyridis*. In 2005, single- and paired-predator assays were tested in the laboratory under simulated early spring and late spring conditions. Digital video recordings were captured every 15 min over 24 h. All species exhibited continuous activity patterns punctuated by longer periods of rest. Predator activity and location did not appear to be coordinated to any particular time of day. Under early spring conditions, *L. nigrinus* had greater activity and a more even behavior distribution than that of *S. tsugae* or *H. axyridis*, which were skewed towards resting. Under late spring conditions, a more even behavioral pattern was seen for the latter two species. Paired-predator assays suggested that conspecifics exert influence on one another, leading to increased dispersal movement and decreased resting, feeding and oviposition. In contrast, heterospecific combinations did not significantly affect behavior patterns. Significant spatial separation was maintained between conspecifics of *L. nigrinus* and *H. axyridis*, and in all heterospecific combinations, supporting our rationale for low-density releases of *Laricobius* adults. Overall, these data suggest that the predators are compatible, as particular temporal and spatial patterns were not coordinated, and avoidance behaviors are likely to keep them from interfering with each other in a field setting. However, the potential negative impacts of conspecifics should be taken into consideration when optimizing mass rearing and release procedures.

The high water-solubility of imidacloprid gives the insecticide desirable efficacy as a systemic insecticide, which is why it is one of the most relied upon insecticides in many insect pest systems. The potential for imidacloprid to be passed through the food chain has not been studied very frequently, and could have many implications for imidacloprid's safety for IPM programs that desire low nontarget impacts to biological control agents, predators, and parasitoids. The effects of systemic application of imidacloprid for control of HWA on its predators, *Laricobius nigrinus* and *Sasajiscymnus tsugae* are being investigated. HWA-infested branches from imidacloprid-treated trees and branches treated in the lab were used as assays for evaluating the impact of the insecticide on the predators. In the lab trials, both species of beetle exhibited a dose-dependent response to imidacloprid doses. Beetles exhibited sublethal effects including tremors and paralysis, and increasing mortality at higher doses. The predators exhibited similar but less pronounced response to feeding on field-treated branches. It appears that imidacloprid can be mediated by the adelgids to predators consuming treated individuals.

SUMMARY OF PHEROMONE LURES OF POTENTIALLY INVASIVE MOTHS (LYMANTRIIDAE: LEPIDOPTERA) AND A RANKING OF THEIR POTENTIAL THREAT TO CERTAIN NORTH AMERICAN HABITATS

Paul W. Schaefer[1] and Gerhard Gries[2]

[1]USDA, Agricultural Research Service,
Beneficial Insects Research Laboratory
501 S. Chapel Street, Newark, DE 19713

[2]Simon Fraser University, Department of Biological Sciences,
8888 University Drive, Burnaby, B.C. V5A 1S6, Canada

ABSTRACT

Many Asian lymantriid moths in the genera *Lymantria* and *Orgyia* pose imminent threats of being accidentally introduced into North America. Based on their (a) extent of polyphagy; (b) potential of transoceanic transportation; (c) likelihood of establishment in North America; and (d) life history traits, we propose a ranked list (descending order) of the 10 most threatening *Lymantria* spp., as follows: *dispar asiatica, monacha, dispar japonica, obfuscata, xylina, lucescens, mathura, fumida, concolor* and *albescens*. Since 1995, we have studied in laboratory analyses and/or field experiments pheromones of these *Lymantria* and some *Orgyia* spp. Based on our findings, synthetic pheromone lures have been, or can be, developed for deployment in surveys for the earliest possible detection of these exotic moths. These (prospective) lures include: (a) (+)–disparlure [(7R,8S)-cis-7,8-epoxy-2-methyloctadecane] for male *Lymantria dispar asiatica, L. japonica, L. albescens, L. atemeles, L. narinda, L. obfuscata,* and *L. concolor*; (b) (+)–disparlure plus (7Z)-2-methyl-7-octadecene for male *L. fumida*; (c) (+)-monachalure [(7R,8S)-cis-7,8-epoxy-octadecane] together with (+)-disparlure and (7Z)-2-methyl-7-octadecene for male *L. monacha*; (d) (+)-xylinalure [(7R,8S)-cis-7,8-epoxy-2-methyleicosane] for male *L. xylina, L. plumbalis* and *L. brunneiplaga*; (e) (+)- and (-)-mathuralure [(9R,10S,3Z,6Z)-cis-9,10-epoxy-3,6-nonadecadiene and (9S,10R,3Z,6Z)-cis-9,10-epoxy-3,6-nonadecadiene] at a 1:4 ratio for male *L. mathura*; (f) bantaizanalure [(7Z,9E)-2-methyl-7,9-octadecadiene] for male *L. bantaizana*; (g) (7Z)-2-methyl-7-octadecene for male *L. lucescens* and *L. iris* (=*L. serva* in Taiwan); (6Z,9Z)-heneicosadien-11-one for male *Teia anartoides*; (h) (6Z)-heneicosen-11-one plus (6Z)-heneicosen-9-one for male *Orgyia thyellina*; and (i) (6Z,9Z)-*trans*-11,12-epoxy-6,9-heneicosadiene for male *O. postica*.

Insofar as habitat susceptibility is concerned, our exercise suggests that temperate mixed oak forests are especially vulnerable to invasion by Asian moths, all AGM's, *L. mathura, L. lucescens*, while larch or spruce forests are vulnerable to *L. monacha* or *L. fumida*. Habitats in Hawaii, S. Calif. or Florida are prime for *L. xylina* and *O. postica*.

CONTROLLING *SIREX NOCTILIO* IN NORTH AMERICA: A NEW PARADIGM

Nathan M. Schiff and A. Dan Wilson

USDA Forest Service, Southern Research Station, Center for Bottomland
Hardwoods Research, P.O. Box 227, Stoneville, MS 38776

ABSTRACT

The *Sirex noctilio* woodwasp, a major pest of North American pines in southern hemisphere countries, recently has entered North America, and become established in the northeast. The spread of *Sirex noctilio* is expected to be rapid. If unchecked it will likely cause significant economic damage to paper and timber industries especially in the southeastern United States. Over the past 50 years, Australian researchers have developed a successful program to control *Sirex noctilio* in *Pinus radiata* plantations utilizing a European nematode, *Beddingia* (=Deladenus) *siricidicola*. We plan to adapt their program to control *Sirex noctilio* in North America, but there are significant differences in ecosystem complexity between North American coniferous forests and southern hemisphere exotic pine monocultures that necessitate further study before this exotic biocontrol agent can be released.

We summarize the differences between southern hemisphere pine ecosystems and North American coniferous forests in Table 1. In the southern hemisphere, there is a single exotic pine species, a single exotic woodwasp, and a single exotic fungal symbiont that helps the woodwasp larvae to feed. In North America, there are at least a dozen native genera of conifers, at least 35 native species of pines, approximately 20 species of native woodwasps, many native wood decay fungi that are associated with conifers, many species of parasitoid wasps and nematodes that attack woodwasps and probably hundreds of native and exotic insects that attack pines. Although, it is clear that the nematode is effective and host specific in simple Australian ecosystems, it is unclear what its nontarget effects might be in North America.

We propose several areas of research including taxonomy, host range testing for the woodwasp, fungus and nematode, interactive effects and fine-tuning different components of the control program such as detection traps, lures and nematode releasing systems (trap trees). Taxonomically, we face problems the Australians do not have to consider. They only have a single exotic woodwasp, whereas we have to differentiate the pest from 20 similar native species. We are in the process of developing a field guide to adult woodwasps and a DNA barcode key to identify larvae. Host range testing is also more complicated than in Australia because of our native diversity. Currently, we are studying the ability of the fungal symbiont to decay different conifer species, and the ability of the nematode to survive on native wood decay fungi. We are also testing interactions between host trees, fungal symbionts, nontarget insects and the nematode. We believe a control program utilizing the nematode is our best chance of successfully controlling *Sirex noctilio* in North America. Our goal is to ensure that it is also the safest.

Table 1.–Comparison of diversity in southern hemisphere pine plantations and North American coniferous habitats.

Southern Hemisphere countries	*North America*
Monoculture of exotic NA pine	Mixed coniferous forests
Single exotic pest, *Sirex noctilio*	20 native siricid species
Few, if any, pine-feeding insects?	Many native conifer-feeding insects
A few exotic parasitoids	Many native parasitoids
One exotic nematode	A few native nematodes
One exotic fungal symbiont	A few native fungal symbionts
Few native wood-decay fungi on pine	Many native wood-decay fungi on pine

POTENTIAL PRODUCTION OF EMERALD ASH BORER ADULTS: TREE, SITE AND LANDSCAPE-LEVEL APPLICATIONS

Nathan W. Siegert and Deborah G. McCullough

Depts. of Entomology & Forestry, Michigan State University,
243 Natural Science Bldg., East Lansing, MI, 48824-1115

ABSTRACT

Emerald ash borer (*Agrilus planipennis* Fairmaire; Coleoptera: Buprestidae), a phloem-feeding beetle native to Asia, was identified in June 2002 as the cause of widespread ash (*Fraxinus* spp.) mortality in forest and urban settings in southeastern lower Michigan and Windsor, Ontario. To date, 21 Michigan counties have been quarantined for emerald ash borer and localized outlier populations have been found across much of lower Michigan. Outlier populations are also established in areas of Indiana, Ohio and Ontario. Regulatory officials and managers of forest land near emerald ash borer infestations must be able to compare alternative management strategies to allocate limited funds efficiently and effectively. In this study, we used empirical data to develop models to estimate phloem area and potential production of emerald ash borer adults in ash trees of varying diameter. In trees killed by emerald ash borer, an average of 101.2 ± 5.49 adult beetles emerged per m^2 of phloem area. Models were applied to ash tree inventory data collected at two outlier sites in Michigan. Results showed that large trees (≥ 43 cm DBH) accounted for less than 5 percent of the ash trees but would have contributed 20-40 percent of the total emerald ash borer adult beetle production at each site. While approximately 80 percent of the trees at the two outlier sites were small (≤ 13 cm DBH), these trees would have accounted for less than 10 percent of the total emerald ash borer adult beetle production. Potential emerald ash borer production in relation to selectively harvesting ash trees in different size classes or conducting sanitation cuts of varying area sizes were discussed. Our results, in combination with ash inventory data, can be used by regulatory officials and forest resource managers to compare options for reducing emerald ash borer density and slowing its rate of spread for any area of interest.

RECONSTRUCTING THE TEMPORAL AND SPATIAL DYNAMICS OF EMERALD ASH BORER ADULTS THROUGH DENDROCHRONOLOGICAL ANALYSES

Nathan W. Siegert[1], Deborah G. McCullough[1], Andrew M. Liebhold[2] and Frank W. Telewski[3]

[1]Depts. of Entomology & Forestry, Michigan State University
243 Natural Science Bldg., East Lansing, MI, 48824-1115

[2]USDA Forest Service, Northeastern Research Station
180 Canfield Street, Morgantown, WV, 26505

[3]Dept. of Plant Biology, Michigan State University
166 Plant Biology Bldg., East Lansing, MI, 48824-1312

ABSTRACT

Emerald ash borer (*Agrilus planipennis* Fairmaire; Coleoptera: Buprestidae) was identified in June 2002 as the cause of widespread ash (*Fraxinus* spp.) mortality in southeastern lower Michigan and Windsor, Ontario. Localized outlier populations have since been discovered across much of lower Michigan and in areas of Indiana, Ohio and Ontario. Two case studies were presented to illustrate how we are using dendrochronological techniques to date when infestations began and to evaluate the subsequent spread and dispersal of emerald ash borer at outlier sites. Preliminary results indicate that the majority of outlier emerald ash borer infestations were established prior to 2002 and that the rate of spread in recently established populations tends to be between 0.1 and 0.2 miles per year, but can be up to 0.4 miles per year under certain conditions (e.g. fragmented urban settings). We are additionally using tree ring analyses to reconstruct the historical dispersal patterns and rates of spread of emerald ash borer throughout the core emerald ash borer infestation in southeastern lower Michigan. Increment cores or cross-sections from emerald ash borer-killed ash trees were preferentially collected over declining or non-stressed ash trees on at least a 3.0 × 3.0 mile sampling grid over an area greater than 5800 mi^2 encompassing the core emerald ash borer infestation. To date, increment cores and cross-sections have been prepared using standard dendrochronological techniques. Crossdating and other dendrochronological analyses are in progress that will reveal when and where emerald ash borer initially became established in southeastern lower Michigan and how it spread historically.

EXPANSION OF THE AMERICAN ELM RESTORATION EFFORT TO THE UPPER MIDWEST

James M. Slavicek

USDA Forest Service, 359 Main Road, Delaware, OH

ABSTRACT

The Forestry Sciences Laboratory, Northeastern Research Station, initiated a project in 2003 to restore the American elm in the state of Ohio. This effort has been expanded to the upper Midwest through establishment of a restoration site in Decorah, IA, Eagle Island, WI, and Hastings, MN. These three sites were established in June of 2005. The sites in Iowa and Minnesota were former farm fields that have been partially planted with trees and are being allowed to naturally evolve. The Wisconsin site is an island that had been reconstructed by the U.S. Army Corps of Engineers. The island contains small sapling trees and grasses were planted in 2003. The effort in these states is being carried out in partnership with Luther College in Iowa, the Army Corps of Engineers in Minnesota, Carpenter St. Croix Nature Center in Minnesota, and the Northeastern Area State and Private Forestry. American elm tree strains with high levels of tolerance to Dutch elm disease (DED) were established in areas where the trees can naturally regenerate and spread. The process of regeneration will allow the American elm to co-evolve with the DED fungal pathogen to ensure this valuable tree species will not be lost from the American landscape. Eight restoration sites have been established to date: in Ohio at the Mohican-Memorial State Forest, Ashland County; Maumee State Forest, Henry County; Highbanks Metro Park, Delaware County; Glacier Ridge Metro Park, Union County; and The Wilds, Muskingum County, and in the new states described above.

PRODUCTION OF LDMNPV IN THE WAVE®
CELL CULTURE BIOREACTOR

James M. Slavicek and J. Matt Gabler

USDA Forest Service, 359 Main Road, Delaware, OH

ABSTRACT

The development of bioreactor production methods for Gypchek would provide a means of production that can be scaled to a large capacity (production of 20,000 acre equivalents + per year), that is potentially at a lower cost than the current larval based production method, and would generate a product completely free of bacteria, fungi, and other viruses. Recently, a bioreactor with a completely novel design was developed and has become the bioreactor of choice by pharmaceutical companies using insect cell lines to produce proteins. This bioreactor, termed the Wave bioreactor, has several advantages compared to a stirred tank bioreactor that include an overall simpler system, elimination of down time between production runs, elimination of autoclave based sterilization, lower production costs, elimination of sheer stress, and potentially greater levels of polyhedra production. The Wave bioreactor system uses a sterile disposable plastic bag (shaped like a pillow) in place of a glass or stainless steel tank to hold the medium and insect cells. The bag is placed on a flat platform, inflated by an air pump, liquid medium and cells are added, and the platform is rocked in a front to back motion. Overall, the Wave bioreactor is a far simpler system than a stirred tank bioreactor because the tank and all stainless steel piping/fittings are eliminated.

The rocking motion of the Wave bioreactor platform creates a wave in the liquid medium that moves back and forth in the bag. The movement of liquid coupled with the large air-fluid interface area allows for significantly greater oxygen transfer than what occurs in stirred tank bioreactors. Consequently, there is no need for an agitator to mix the fluid within the Wave bag, or a sparger to bubble air/oxygen through the medium. The agitator and sparger in stirred tank bioreactors cause shear stress on the insect cells. Elimination of shear stress caused by the agitator and sparger should result in healthier cells and greater polyhedra production. Methods to produce Gypchek in the Wave bioreactor will be developed and we will determine whether the Wave or a stirred tank bioreactor is best for virus production. Results to date indicate that the Wave bioreactor virtually eliminates shear stress based on the condition of the cells. Cells in the Wave were free from granular material and vacuoles. In contrast, most of the cells within a stirred tank bioreactor contain vacuoles and granular material after 4-5 days. In addition, in contrast to a stirred tank bioreactor cells can be grown in the Wave system without pluronic F-68.

IMPACT OF EMERALD ASH BORER ON FORESTS WITHIN THE HURON RIVER WATERSHED OF SOUTHEAST MICHIGAN

Annemarie Smith[1], Daniel A. Herms[2] and Robert P. Long[3]

[1]The Ohio State University, Environmental Science
Graduate Program, 400 Aronoff Laboratory,
318 W. 12th Street, Columbus, OH 43210

[2]Department of Entomology, The Ohio State University,
Ohio Agricultural Research and Development Center,
1680 Madison Avenue, Wooster, OH 44691

[3]USDA Forest Service, 359 Main Road, Delaware, OH 43015

ABSTRACT

Emerald ash borer (*Agrilus planipennis* Fairmaire) (EAB), a buprestid beetle native to Asia, has killed millions of ash trees (*Fraxinus* spp.) over thousands of square miles in southeast Michigan, northwest Ohio and neighboring Ontario. This invasive pest has the potential to decimate ash across North America with major impacts on forest ecosystems.

The objectives of this study were to determine (1) if community structure affects forest susceptibility to EAB invasion; and (2) the effects of EAB-induced ash mortality on forest community composition. Transects were established in 31 forested stands in southeast Michigan that varied in ash density, topography, hydrology, stand structure, and community composition. Three replicated ¼-acre plots were established in each transect for quantification of overstory and understory woody vegetation. The impact of EAB was quantified by assessing crown dieback of each ash tree and counting the characteristic D-shaped emergence holes of the beetles and woodpecker attacks at a standard location on the trunk of each ash tree.

We found no relationship between EAB-induced dieback or mortality of ash and density, basal area, relative dominance, or relative density of ash. Severity of ash dieback was negatively correlated with distance of the stand from the putative epicenter of the invasion. Black ash (*F. nigra*) dieback was greater than that of white (*F. americana*) or green ash (*F. pennsylvanica*). As EAB eliminates ash from infested stands, abundance of saplings and seedlings suggests that *Acer* (maple), *Ulmus* (elm), *Tilia* (basswood) and *Prunus* (cherry) are most likely to replace ash in the canopy.

Each stand has been spatially referenced via GPS to facilitate long-term monitoring of successional trajectories and other ecological impacts, which are important to understand so consequences of the EAB invasion can be mitigated if efforts to contain the spread of EAB are unsuccessful.

DETECTION AND MONITORING OF EMERALD ASH BORER POPULATIONS: TRAP TREES AND THE FACTORS THAT MAY INFLUENCE THEIR EFFECTIVENESS

Andrew J. Storer[1], Jessica A. Metzger[1], Ivich Fraser[2], Deborah G. McCullough[3], Therese M. Poland[4] and Robert L. Heyd[5]

[1]School of Forest Resources and Environmental Science, Michigan Technological University, 1400 Townsend Drive, Houghton, MI 49931
[2]USDA, APHIS, PPQ Emerald Ash Borer Project, 5936 Ford Ct., Suite 200 Brighton, MI 48116
[3]Departments of Entomology and Forestry, Michigan State University, East Lansing, MI 48824
[4]USDA Forest Service, North Central Research Station, East Lansing, MI 48823
[5]Forestry, Fire and Mineral Management Division
Michigan Department of Natural Resources, Marquette, MI 49855

ABSTRACT

The exotic emerald ash borer (EAB), *Agrilus planipennis* Fairmaire, was first identified in Michigan in 2002, though it had likely been established there for a number of years prior to detection. A key to management of EAB populations is the ability to detect this insect in order to accurately describe its distribution and to locate new outlier populations. A number of detection tools have been tested, and the mostly widely implemented to date has been the use of trap trees. Trap trees consist of ash trees which have been intentionally girdled with the goal of making them more attractive to EAB. Adult EAB may be trapped on a sticky surface on the tree, or larvae may be detected by peeling the tree after possible exposure to adults. In this presentation we provide an overview of the reasons that trap trees are used, what influences their success in detecting EAB, and the surveys that utilize this technique. We summarize the findings of experiments conducted from 2003 to 2005.

EAB lands more frequently on unwounded ash trees than on unwounded trees of other species in a stand, though some landing does occur on other species. Girdling ash trees generally makes them more attractive than ungirdled trees, passive flight traps or flight traps baited with host material in the form of crushed leaves or scorched branches. However, there are some inconsistencies in results from different studies comparing girdled and ungirdled trees.

Trap trees are apparently effective as a result of the stress and potentially associated stress volatiles induced by girdling the tree rather than a result of the wound itself or host volatiles associated with the wound. Studies have investigated the attractiveness of trap trees related to stress induction method, year of girdling, season of girdling, position of the girdled tree in the forest canopy, position of the trapping surface relative to the girdling wound and position of the girdling wound on the tree. Results of these experiments are variable, and may be related to the population density of the insect at the sites where the tests were carried out.

In both 2004 and 2005, the Michigan Department of Agriculture utilized more than 10,000 girdled trap trees throughout Michigan to detect outlier populations of EAB. All of these trees were cut at the end of the flight season and peeled to look for developing larvae. Risk-based trap tree EAB detection surveys were conducted in 2004 and 2005 by Michigan Technological University in collaboration with the USDA Forest Service and Michigan Department of Natural Resources. These surveys focused on areas into which firewood was likely to have been moved and included 116 sites in 2004 and 161 sites in 2005 in Michigan and northern Wisconsin. A subset of these trees was peeled at the end of the season, with the remainder left standing in order to be reused the subsequent year. In 2005, at some sites in the latter survey, trees that were girdled in 2004 and left standing were more effective as traps than tress girdled in 2005 at the start of the trapping season. Both surveys resulted in detection of outlier populations of EAB.

There is clearly a need for improved understanding of trap tree efficacy and EAB population levels they are able to detect. Further integration of trap tree technologies with other trapping and detection techniques is needed. In the meantime, trap trees remain one of the most effective tools for detecting EAB.

NONTARGET IMPACT OF *BACILLUS THURINGIENSIS KURSTAKI* IN CENTRAL APPALACHIAN MIXED BROADLEAF-PINE FORESTS: LONG-TERM EVALUATION OF ARTHROPODS

John S. Strazanac, George E. Seidel, Vicki Kondo, Cynthia J. Fritzler and Linda Butler

Plant and Soil Sciences / Entomology,
West Virginia University, Morgantown, WV

ABSTRACT

Current measures for gypsy moth (*Lymantria dispar* L.) control emphasize the use of pheromones, growth regulators, and biopesticides. One of the biopesticides, *Bacillus thuringiensis kurstaki* (*Btk*), will continue to be necessary for immediate control of gypsy moth and other forest lepidopteran outbreaks. Although *Btk* can be a highly effective control for gypsy moth and other forest lepidopteran pests, it is recognized to affect a wide array of foliage feeding lepidopterans. Natural enemies of spring caterpillars may also be indirectly impacted.

A 7-year field study of the nontarget impacts from applications of *Btk* to control gypsy moth is summarized. *Btk* treatments caused significant declines of lepidopterans, but *Btk's* impact was dependent on the caterpillar stage being exposed through feeding on treated foliage. Some indirect impacts on natural enemies of caterpillars directly impacted *Btk* treatments were also significant. Recovery of caterpillars significantly impacted by *Btk* to pretreatment levels required as much as 2 years.

DETECTION OF THE BROWN SPRUCE LONGHORN BEETLE, *TETROPIUM FUSCUM* (F.) WITH SEMIOCHEMICAL-BAITED TRAPS, TREE BANDS, AND VISUAL SURVEYS

Jon Sweeney[1], Jessica Price[1], Wayne MacKay[1],
Bob Guscott[2], Peter de Groot[3] and Jerzy Gutowski[4]

[1]Natural Resources Canada, Canadian Forest Service, Fredericton, NB
[2]Nova Scotia Department of Natural Resources, Shubenacadie, NS
[3]Natural Resources Canada, Canadian Forest Service, Sault Ste. Marie, ON
[4]Forest Research Institute, Białowieża, Poland

ABSTRACT

The brown spruce longhorn beetle, *Tetropium fuscum* (F.) (Coleoptera: Cerambycidae), (BSLB) native to northern and central Europe, has been the focus of a containment and eradication program by the Canadian Food Inspection Agency in the city of Halifax, Nova Scotia, since May 2000. Surveys are conducted using host volatile-baited traps and visual ground surveys. Detection of BSLB-infested trees is done mainly by visual inspection of stems for typical signs of infestation, such as excessive resin flow or characteristic elliptical exit holes about 4 mm in diameter. In the first couple of years of the BSLB survey and eradication program, there were many trees with obvious signs of infestation, likely caused by several years of re-infestation. Most such trees have been removed and the challenge now is to detect the presence of BSLB in trees with less obvious signs of infestation. Some infested hosts such as windfelled trees and freshly cut logs do not display resinosis. It is also possible that the presence or extent of resin flow on the bole varies with species (e.g., *Picea rubens* vs. *P. glauca*) and level of moisture stress. If this is true, then these hosts could be missed in visual surveys. Guscott (unpublished data) showed that burlap bands wrapped around the stem of "suspect" infested trees were useful at

BSLB adults. In 2004, as part of a field experiment testing *Beauveria bassiana* for infection of BSLB adults, we found that a band of polyester quilt batting wrapped around a spruce trunk was very effective at trapping BSLB adults. The present study was conducted to determine the accuracy of visual surveys for detection of BSLB-infested trees and to test relationships in BSLB population estimates obtained from visual surveys, polyester tree bands, volatile-baited traps, and destructive sampling.

In early May 2005, a total of 151 white spruce trees larger than 10 cm DBH were selected (by coin toss) in five plots (30-31 trees per plot) on McNabs Island located in Halifax harbor. Each tree was tagged, numbered, and wrapped at breast height with a 20-cm-wide band of polyester quilt batting to act as a trap for foraging adult BSLB. Two Intercept™ – PT (Advanced Pheromone Technologies Inc.) traps, each baited with an ultra high release (UHR) rate BSLB kairomone lure and UHR ethanol lure (PheroTech) were hung 30 m apart on opposite sides of each plot. Quilt bands and volatile-baited traps were checked for adult BSLB every 2 weeks until late August. In late summer each sample tree was "blindly" inspected by an operational survey crew from the Canadian

Food Inspection Agency (CFIA) and designated as BSLB-positive or negative, based on typical signs of infestation, e.g., unexplained resin flow on the stem or characteristic exit holes. In mid-October, all 151 trees were felled and a 5-ft-long basal log collected for destructive sampling. A 4-ft-section of each basal log was milled into 1-cm-thick slabs to expose mature BSLB larvae in pupal cells; the remaining 1-ft-long bolt was incubated at 20-22 °C for 12 weeks to rear out adult BSLB. Data on BSLB infestation of individual trees from the destructive samples (slabbing, rearing) were compared with that predicted from quilt bands and visual signs to determine the number and percentage of false negatives (failure to detect an infested tree) and false positives (falsely designated an uninfested trees as BSLB-infested).

Volatile-baited traps captured BSLB adults in all five plots. Quilt bands detected BSLB adults on 38 of 151 trees with numbers per band ranging from 1 to 20. CFIA inspectors designated 17 of 151 trees as BSLB-infested based on visual signs. The destructive samples indicated that only 7 of 151 trees (5%) were infested with BSLB. The numbers of adults per quilt band was positively related to: 1) the number of larvae per tree (in the basal log); and 2) tree diameter. All seven infested trees were included in the BSLB-positive trees detected by visual inspection and quilt bands, i.e., neither method missed infested trees, both scored 0 percent false negatives. On the other hand, visual inspection and quilt bands falsely designated 10 (7%) and 28 trees (19%), respectively, as BSLB positive. Too many false positives can waste time and money for unnecessary tree removal. However, when surveying for a quarantine pest, failing to detect an infested tree (false negative) is far more serious an error than mistakenly declaring an uninfested tree as infested (false positive), so in this regard both survey methods performed well. A similar survey was conducted at five sites near the edge of the BSLB quarantine zone where BSLB populations are much lower and more difficult to detect but results will not be known until destructive sampling is completed in February 2006.

CONTROL OF ASIAN CYCAD SCALE ON *CYCAS REVOLUTA* AND *C. TAITUNGENSIS* USING IMICIDE TRUNK MICROINJECTION

Terry A. Tattar[1] and Arnold Farran[2]

[1]Professor Emeritus, Dept. of Microbiology,
University of Massachusetts, Amherst, MA 01002

[2]Director of Research, J. J. Mauget Company, Arcadia, CA 91006

ABSTRACT

Asian cycad scale is native to Thailand and southern China but was imported to Florida on nursery stock. This insect has since spread on imported cycads to Guam, Hawaii and Puerto Rico where it poses a threat to native cycads in tropical forests. In 2005, the Asian cycad scale had already infested native cycads throughout the forests of Guam, many of which are *C. micornesica* that are over 100 years old. Mortality of 100 percent of cycads can be expected within 1 year following infestation of the Asian cycad scale. This insect has also caused serious losses in nursery cycad stock and in cycad landscape plantings in California, Florida, and Puerto Rico. Control of this insect by spray applications has not been effective. Application of Imicide, a 10 percent imidacloprid formulation, via trunk injection from 3 ml Mauget capsules was investigated in a mature cycad planting in southern California. Asian cycad scale populations were reduced in Imicide-injected cycads by 32 percent after 60 days while scale populations increased by 268 percent in untreated control cycads.

References

DOACS, DPI. (March 2000). *Cycad aulacaspis scale, Aulacaspis yasumatsui.* http://www.doacs.state.fl.us/~pi/enpp/ento/aulacaspis.html (11 July 2000)

Donnegan, J. A., S. L. Butler, et al. (2004). **Guam's forest resources, 2002**. http://www.fs.fed.us/pnw/pubs/pnw_rb243.pdf

Hill, K., 1998, **The Cycad Pages.** Royal Botanic Gardens, Sydney, Australia

Howard FW, Hamon A, McLaughlin M, Weissling T. 1999. *Aulacaspis yasumatsui* **(Homoptera: *Sternorrhyncha*: *Diaspididae*), a scale insect pest of cycads recently introduced into Florida.** Florida Entomologist 82: 14 - 27.

McLaughlin, M. (1998). **What's this white stuff on my cycad**. http://www.ftg.org/horticulture/n_cycadscale.html

Moore, A., I. Iriarte and R. Quitugua. 2005. **Asian cycad scale, *Aulacaspis yasumatsui* Takagi. Pest Sheet 2005-01**. Co-op Ext. Serv. University of Guam.

Takagi S. 1977. **A new species of Aulacaspis associated with a cycad in Thailand** (Homoptera: Cocoidea). Insecta Matsumurana New Series 11:63-72.

Tattar, T.A., and A. Farran. 2004. **Asian cycad Scale: new threat to cycads. a new threat tocycads.** Irrigation and Green Industry 7:50-55 (2004).

Whitelock , L. M., 2002, **The Cycads,** Timber Press, Portland, Oregon.

MULTI-YEAR EVALUATION OF MATING DISRUPTION TREATMENTS AGAINST GYPSY MOTH

Patrick C. Tobin[1], Kevin W. Thorpe[2] and Laura M. Blackburn[1]

[1]USDA Forest Service, Northern Research Station,
180 Canfield Street, Morgantown, WV

[2]USDA ARS, Insect Biocontrol Laboratory, Room 319, Beltsville, MD

ABSTRACT

Mating disruption is the use of synthetic pheromone flakes that are aerially applied to foliage with the goal of interfering with male gypsy moths' ability to locate females and mate. Mating disruption is the primary tactic against gypsy moth used in the Gypsy Moth Slow-the-Spread Project (STS) [Tobin et al. 2004. *Amer. Entomol.* 50:200]. Since 1996, over 1.8 million acres have been treated using this tactic, which accounts for ≈75% of all the acreage treated in STS (Decision Support for the STS Project, *http://da.ento.vt.edu*). We were motivated by preliminary field data that suggested residual flakes from previous treatments may obfuscate our interpretation of the effect of this tactic. We thus explored historical STS treatment data, from 1996-2004, to determine if there was a pattern that would suggest potential residual effects of mating disruption.

We first conducted preliminary field studies in 2004 and 2005 to determine if there were biological effects from residual pheromone flakes in the years after treatment. In both years, we observed a reduction in male moth capture in plots previously treated with pheromone flakes relative to an untreated control, while plots treated in the current year still showed the greatest reduction in trap catch. This is of critical concern in STS since treatment evaluation is based on moth abundance in the year after treatment. If residual pheromone flakes are present, then we are potentially overestimating the effect of this tactic, and more importantly, we are potentially underestimating the abundance of the gypsy moth colony that we are attempting to eradicate.

In STS, the efficacy of treatments is evaluated through an Index of Treatment Success [Sharov et al. 2002. *J. Econ. Entomol.* 95:1205], T1, which is based on the philosophy of Abbott's formula [Abbott 1925. *J. Econ. Entomol.* 18:265]. It considers the population abundance in the treatment block before and after treatment, while adjusting for the respective change in population in nearby, untreated areas that serve as a "control." In our analysis, we expanded T1, the Index of Treatment Evaluation, to include two additional indices, T2 and T3, that measure the potential effects of mating disruption treatments up to 2 years after application:

T1 – Measures changes in moth density 1 year before and 1 year after treatment. Currently the STS treatment evaluation standard.

T2 – Measures changes in moth density 1 year before and 2 years after treatment.

T3 – Measures changes in moth density 1 year after and 2 years after treatment.

A total of 250 mating disruption blocks across the gypsy moth transition zone were examined from 1996 to 2004. Based on the respective behavior of T1, T2, and T3, there were four principle patterns:

PATTERN 1. T1, T2, and T3 indices all suggested a successful application of the mating disruption treatment, which was seen in 120 of the 250 blocks. In these blocks, the population in the treated area declined following treatment, and remained low 2 years later. This is the desired outcome of the STS program when treatments are deployed.

PATTERN 2. T1, the current STS standard, suggested an unsuccessful treatment, while T2 and T3 suggested a successful application. This pattern was seen in only 11 of 250 blocks, and could be indicative of a scenario in which residual pheromone flakes interfered with mating finding in the year after initial application, thereby leading to a continual reduction in abundance.

PATTERN 3. T1 and T2 suggested treatment success, but T3 suggested failure. This was seen in only 19 of 250 blocks. This could be indicative of some effect of residual pheromone flakes, which resulted in decreased male moth abundance 1 year following treatment; however, it remains unclear if some part of this reduction was due to an underestimate of the male moth abundance.

PATTERN 4. T1, the current STS standard, suggested a successful treatment, while T2 and T3 suggested a failure. This was seen in 100 of the 250 blocks, and represents the most problematic pattern. In this pattern, we have overestimated the long-term efficacy of our treatment, and/or potentially underestimated, due to interference from residual flakes, moth abundance after treatment. It is noteworthy that 2 years following treatment, mean moth density in treated blocks was similar to those in nearby, untreated blocks.

The deployment of mating disruption tactics against gypsy moth under STS is the largest such program in the world, and hence could serve as a paradigm for the development of related insect pest management programs. These results could effectively alter our current method of evaluating the efficacy of mating disruption. They also pose interesting biological questions regarding the degree towards which residual pheromone flakes in the environment alter moth behavior. We are currently examining historical STS treatment data for residual effects up to 3 years following treatment. We also plan to compare these results with blocks treated with *Bacillus thuringiensis kurstaki*, which is the second most used gypsy moth management tactic in STS and one in which there are little, if any, residual effects.

THE EFFECTS OF CLIMATE, GEOGRAPHY, AND TIME ON HEMLOCK WOOLLY ADELGID AND ITS NATURAL ENEMIES

R. Talbot Trotter, III

USDA Forest Service, Northeastern Center for Forest Health Research
51 Mill Pond Road, Hamden, CT 06514

ABSTRACT

Although the hemlock woolly adelgid (HWA) has been documented in the western United States since the 1920s, it has not expressed outbreak dynamics, and has not behaved as a pest species. In the eastern United States however, the spatial and temporal dynamics of the HWA have been quite different. First observed in the east in 1951 in Richmond, VA, the HWA has rapidly expanded its range, and is now found from southern Maine to northern Georgia. This rapid range expansion threatens the health and sustainability of the eastern and Carolina hemlock (*Tsuga canadensis*, and *T. caroliniana*, respectively) in the east. Effective management of this species through biocontrol programs demands a solid understanding of the spatial and temporal factors influencing the dynamics of both the HWA, and the natural enemies used for biocontrol.

County records providing the first year in which HWA infestations were documented provide an opportunity to describe the coarse, large-scale movement of HWA through the distribution of hemlock. Spatial projections of these records as a time series show that early reports of HWA appear spatially disjunct, with new reported populations appearing in noncontiguous locations at significant distances from those previously infested. These early records suggest a number of scenarios including: 1) inadvertent anthropogenic movement of HWA populations; 2) early lack of experience with, and knowledge of, HWA by land managers and the general public resulted in failure to detect populations at the time of their arrival, which produced a lag between arrival and detection; 3) incomplete records; and 4) some combination of these (and/or other) factors. Yet, despite the apparent spatial discontinuity of early populations, more recent records (1991-2004) of HWA, collected with improved detection and documentation, suggest a more continuous and regular expansion of HWA populations through hemlock forests.

Although this more recent expansion has been more contiguous, variation in the rates and directions of expansion suggest the interaction between landscape features and climate have produced "barriers" and "windows" which may inhibit or facilitate the spread of this species. The most apparent of these barriers is that produced by the cold temperatures in the high elevations along the Appalachian Mountain Range. Prior to 1998, populations of HWA were predominantly restricted to the eastern edge of this range. Previous work (Parker et al. 1997, 1999) has shown that HWA may be limited by cold tolerance. However, during 1998, populations of HWA became established along the western edge of the Appalachians, and have rapidly expanded through previously uninfested regions. Compilation of climate date throughout the eastern United States shows that the winter of 1998 and the following two winters were anomalously warm. The interaction between the landscape (via altitude driven cold temperatures), climate, and timing of HWA spread suggest the climate, specifically a warm period, opened a temporal window in a landscape driven temperature barrier. By exploiting these landscape patterns, we can begin to define the potential biogeographic limits to HWA populations, based on current and potential climate conditions.

SPATIAL AND TEMPORAL DISTRIBUTION OF IMIDACLOPRID IN EASTERN HEMLOCK

Richard M. Turcotte

USDA Forest Service, Forest Health Protection,
180 Canfield Street, Morgantown, WV 26505

ABSTRACT

Enzyme-linked immunosorbent assay (ELISA) and gas chromatography/mass spectrometry (GC/MS) techniques were used to measure imidacloprid and metabolite concentrations in xylem fluid extracted from eastern hemlock (*Tsuga canadensis*) trees treated in the spring or fall with soil or trunk applications of the systemic insecticides Merit® 2F and IMA-jet® (5%). Background chemical interferences in ELISA, were eliminated by a 1:20 dilution of extracts with water. Xylem fluid samples were collected from 64 eastern hemlock trees at each of two sites. These samples were collected at 3, 6, 9, 12, and 15 weeks after treatment from within the crown. Twelve branches within the crown representing three heights and four cardinal directions were clipped and xylem fluid extracted using a pressure chamber. To date, imidacloprid and its metabolites have only been detected in the xylem fluid of trees whose trunk was injected with IMA-jet®. Imidacloprid initially detected at 3 weeks, has sustained levels through 15 weeks of sampling. Height and cardinal direction did not appear to effect results through there was considerable variability among samples.

BACILLUS THURINGIENSIS TOXINS TRIGGER RECEPTOR SHEDDING FROM GYPSY MOTH MIDGUT CELLS

Algimantas P. Valaitis

USDA Forest Service, 359 Main Road,
Delaware, OH 43015

ABSTRACT

The mechanism of action of the Cry1 insecticidal proteins produced by *Bacillus thuringiensis* (Bt) begins with the processing of these proteins in the larval gut. After proteolytic activation, the Bt toxins bind to specific midgut receptors and insert into the membrane of the gut epithelial cells, causing insect death. Aminopeptidases, cadherins, other proteins and glycoconjugates have been found to function as Bt toxin receptors in different insect species. However, what happens after the toxin-receptor interaction remains controversial. Based on earlier studies it was proposed that the Bt toxins form pores that cause cell swelling and death by colloidal osmotic lysis. More recent studies suggest that the binding of the Bt toxin to its receptor induces an aberrant signal transduction response that kills the gut cells. In this study we looked at the fate of aminopeptidase N (APN) in gypsy moth larvae after challenge with Bt toxins and secondary messengers including AMP and cyclic AMP. Bt toxins induced rapid shedding of APN from the gut epithelial cells in a dose- and time-dependent manner. Moreover, the release of APN was also induced by AMP but was blocked by administering cyclic AMP along with the toxin. These findings show that Bt toxins trigger receptor shedding and suggest an involvement of a secondary messenger signaling pathway in the dysfunction and death of the intestinal epithelial cells.

EVALUATION OF NON-NATIVE *TSUGA* SPECIES AS REPLACEMENTS FOR *T. CANADENSIS* KILLED BY HEMLOCK WOOLLY ADELGID

Paul A. Weston[1] and Richard W. Harper[2]

[1]Department of Entomology, Cornell University, 150 Insectary, Ithaca, NY 14853

[2]Cornell Cooperative Extension of Westchester Co., 26 Legion Dr., Valhalla, NY 10595

ABSTRACT

Several species of *Tsuga* from the western United States and Asia are under evaluation as potential replacements for *T. canadensis* being destroyed by hemlock woolly adelgid (*Adelges tsugae* Annand). Test plots were established in Katonah, NY in October, 2003, and trees were inoculated with adelgid egg masses in spring of 2004 and 2005. Adelgids have yet to establish on test trees, but dramatic differences in tree growth among the species is apparent. *T. canadensis* and *T. chinensis* have shown the largest growth increment, while the remaining test species have shown almost no growth over an 18-month period. *T. chinensis*, in addition to being a vigorous grower, has botanical traits much like *T. canadensis*, which leads to the preliminary conclusion that this species might be a suitable replacement for *T. canadensis* and/or *T. caroliniana*, pending evaluation of its susceptibility to hemlock woolly adelgid (reports in the literature indicate that it is resistant).

PHYTOEXTRACTION OF LEAD FROM FIRING RANGE SOILS WITH VETIVER GRASS

E.W. Wilde[1], R.L. Brigmon[1], D.L. Dunn[1], M.A. Heitkamp[1] and D.C. Dagnan[2]

[1]Westinghouse Savannah River Company,
Savannah River National Laboratory, Aiken, SC 29808

[2]USDA Forest Service, 11 Campus Blvd., Suite 200,
Newtown Square, PA 19703

ABSTRACT

Vetiver grass (*Vetiveria zizanoides*) along with soil amendments were evaluated for phytoextraction of lead and other metals (zinc, copper, and iron) from the soil of an active firing range at the Savannah River Site, SC. Lead-contaminated soil (300–4,500 ppm/kg) was collected, dried, placed in pots, fertilized, and used as a medium for growing transplanted Vetiver grass plants in a greenhouse. The uptake of metals by the plants was evaluated in response to various fertilization and pre-harvest treatments.

Plants grew better when fertilized with Osmocote fertilizer in comparison to plants fertilized with 10-10-10 (NPK) fertilizer. Application of a chelating agent, EDTA, one week before harvest significantly increased the amount of lead that was extracted. Lead concentrations of up to 1,390–1,450 ppm/kg were detected in tissue samples. Maximum lead levels were observed in root tissues. The addition of nonlethal doses of a slow-release herbicide in combination with EDTA did not appear to significantly enhance phytoextraction or the translocation of lead into shoots.

HEMLOCK WOOLLY ADELGID AND ITS NATURAL ENEMIES IN SICHUAN PROVINCE, CHINA, 2005

Jianhua Zhou[1], Yinbo Xiao[1], Yugui Xiao[1], Wenhua Lu[2],
Michael Montgomery[3], Roy Van Driesche[2] and Scott Salom[4]

[1]Institute of Forest Protection, Sichuan Academy of Forestry,
Chengdu, 610066, China

[2]Department of Plant, Soil, and Insect Sciences, University of Massachusetts
Fernald Hall, Amherst, MA 01003

[3]USDA Forest Service, 51 Millpond Road, Hamden, CT 06514

[4]Department of Entomology, Virginia Tech University, Blacksburg, VA 24601

ABSTRACT

A partnership of Chinese and American institutions was formed in 2005 to obtain natural enemies for biological control of *Adelges tsugae* Annand, the hemlock woolly adelgid (HWA), in the eastern United States. We report here the first 6 months (June-November) of studies done at three sites in Kangding and Baoxing Counties in Sichuan Province. Previously, *Scymnus camptodromus* and *Laricobius* spp. had been collected there for shipment to the United States. The hemlock *Tsuga chinensis* grows at two of the sites and *T. dumosa* at one. Also present are spruce, fir, and five-needle pine, which are attacked by other species of adelgids.
When monitoring of HWA development began in June, both wingless and winged adults of the progrediens generation were present. By late summer, mostly aestivating neosistens nymphs were present, but some egg-laying adults and developing nymphs were also found, suggesting that some neosistens had an abbreviated diapause. HWA distribution in tree crowns was light and uniform; percentages of HWA-infested terminal shoots on the four cardinal directions were 6.0 percent, 7.1 percent, 5.9 percent, and 5.4 percent, with 6.9 percent and 5.2 percent in the lower and upper crown, respectively.

Predator diversity was assessed monthly by beating hemlock and pine foliage over an inverted umbrella. The Coccinellidae was the most speciose (28 species) and abundant (43% of specimens) group of the 1418 specimens and 127 morph species collected. *Scymnus* lady beetles dominated at each site but the dominate species varied; *S. camptodromus* dominated at Nibagou; *S. geminus* and *S. lycotropus* at Simaqiao; *S. ancontophyllus*, *S. camptodromus*, and *S. huashansong* at Yangcanggou. Nibagou had the least diverse and Yancanggou the most diverse guild of Coccinellidae. *S. camptodromus* was found mostly on hemlock, *S. geminus* was found mostly on pine, and *S. lycotropus* was found more on hemlock than pine in June but mostly on pine in July, when HWA was aestivating and adelgids on pine were growing and ovipositing. Another noteworthy family of predators was Anthocoridae (Hemiptera): seven species were found, mostly late in the season.

POSTERS

The Russians are coming—aren't they? Siberian moth in European forests: Baranchikov, YN & Petko, VM

Larch bud gall midges: candidates for an mpty ecological niche on American larches: Baranchikov, YN; Moiseyev, AS & Baigal-Amar, T

Host range of the exotic brown marmorated stink bug, *Halyomorpha halys* (Heteroptera: Pentatomidae); Implications for future distribution: Bernon, GK; Bernhard, KM; Nielsen, AL; Stimme, JF; Hoebeke, ER & Carter, ME

A comparison of strategies for experimentally inoculating eastern hemlock with the hemlock woolly adelgid: Butin, E; Preisser, E & Elkinton, J

Hyperspectral remote sensing and its uses in vegetation management. Cole, J., et al. **Horizontal transmission of the microsporidium *Nosema lymantriae* in gypsy moth larvae:** Hoch, G; D'Amico, V; Solter, L; Zubrik, M; McManus, ML

Multi-year residual activity of Arborjet's IMA-jet (imidacloprid 5% SL) against emerald ash borer [*Agrilus planipennis* Fairemaire (Coleoptera: Buprestidae)] in green ash (*Fraxinus pennsylvanica* Marsh) in Troy, MI: Doccola, JJ; Wild, PM; Bristol, EJ; Lojko, J & Li, X

Their natives are our exotics: International collaboration and outreach through invasive.org: Douce, GK; Moor-head, DJ; Bargeron, CT; Evans, CW & Reardon, RC

The black twig borer, *Xylosandrus compactus* (Coleoptera: Scolytidae): A serious pest of native Hawaiian forest restoration: Dudley, N; Stein, JD; Jones, T & Gillette, NE

An *Ophiostoma* sp. causing a vascular wilt disease of red bay (*Persea borbonia*) is also pathogenic to other species in the Lauraceae family: Fraedrich, S

Effects of host species and population density on Anoplophora glabripennis (Coleoptera: Cerambycidae) flight propensity: Francese, JA; Lance, DR; Wang, B; Xu, Z; Sawyer, AJ & Mastro, VC

Effects of trap design and placement on capture of emerald ash borer, *Agrilus planipennis*: Francese, JA; Oliver, JB; Fraser, I; Youssef, N; Lance, DR; Crook, DJ & Mastro, VC

Interaction between the gypsy moth (*Lymantria dispar* L.) and some competitive defoliators: Glavendekic, MM & Mihajlovic, LS

The gypsy moth event monitor for FVS: A tool for forest and pest managers: Gottschalk, KW & Courter, AW

Do bark beetles and wood borers infest lumber following heat treatment? The role of bark: Haack, RA & Petrice, TR

New associations between the Asian pests *Anoplophora* spp. and local parasitoids, in Italy: Hérard, F; Ciampitti, M; Maspero, M; Cocquempot, C; Delvare, G; Lopez, J & Colombo, M

Novel ectomycorrhizal fungi forming symbiotic association with American chestnut trees: Hiremath, S & Lehtoma, K

Blight-resistant American chestnut trees: Selection of progeny from a breeding program: Hiremath, S; Lehtoma, K & Hebard, F

Biological control of mile-a-minute weed, *Polygonum perfoliatum*: first release of the Chinese weevil, *Rhinoncomimus latipes*: Hough-Goldstein, J

Reproductive behavior of *Anoplophora glabripennis* (Coleoptera: Cerambycidae) in the laboratory: Keena, M & Sanchez, V

Studies of the inheritance of resistance to *Cryptococcus fagisuga* in the American beech: Koch, JL; Larson, RA & Carey, DW

Field transmission of a microsporidian pathogen of gypsy moth, *Lymantria dispar L.*: Kolling, TA & Linde, A

Efficacy of basal soil injection at different water volumes and landscape settings for Asian longhorn beetle control: Lewis, PA

Introducing natural enemies for the management of emerald ash borer in North America: Liu, H & Bauer, L

A comparison of the density and parasitism of armored scales (Hemiptera Diaspididae) on *Tsuga* spp. in Japan and the Northeastern U.S.: Lyon, S; Abell, C; Van Dreische, R; Reardon, R & Kamata, N

Release and monitoring of *Laricobius nigrinus* (Coleoptera: Derodontidae) for classical biological control of HWA in the eastern U.S.: Mausel, DL; Salom, SM & Kok, LT

Chemical ecology, fungal interactions, and forest stand correlations of an exotic ambrosia beetle, *Xylosandrus crassiusculus*: Ott, EP; Sullivan, BT; Klepzig, KD & Schowalter, TD

Adaptation during northern range expansion in the elongate hemlock scale, *Fiorinia externa*: Preisser, E; Lodge, A; Orwig, D & Elkinton, J

Responses of the emerald ash borer, *Agrilus planipennis*, to induced plant volatiles: Rodriguez-Saona, C; Poland, T; Grant, G; de Groot, P; Buchan, L; Stelinski, L; MacDonald, L & Miller, J

Methods for dating injury caused by the Asian longhorned beetle, *Anoplophora glabripennis*: Sawyer, AJ; Panagakios, WS & Kreuz, SM

Life tables for the Asian longhorned beetle on its principal hosts in the US: Sawyer, AJ; Panagakios, WS & Kreuz, SM

Summary of pheromone lures of potentially invasive moths (Lepidoptera: Lymantriidae) and a ranking of their potential threat to certain North American habitats: Schaefer, PW & Gries, G

Production of LdNPV in the wave cell culture bioreactor: Slavicek, JM & Gabler, J

Expansion of the American elm restoration effort to the upper Midwest: Slavicek, J

The impact of emerald ash borer on forests within the Huron River Watershed: Smith, A; Herms, DA & Long, RP

Sentinel/trap trees for Asian longhorned beetle: Smith, MT; Wu, JQ; He, WZ & Zhong, GL

Slow release encapsulated contact insecticide for Asian longhorned beetle: Implications for detection, attract-and-kill and population suppression: Smith, MT; Wu, JQ; Tropp, J; Wu, JQ & He, WZ

Asian longhorned beetle cooperative eradication program: Stefan, M; Markham, C; Twardowski, J & Bond, S

Electrophysiological Bt assays: Fundamental tenets tested: Steiger, DB; D'Amico, V & Keil, C

Rapid spread of the horse chestnut leaf-miner (*Cameraria ohridella* Deschka & Dimic) in the UK: Straw, N; Tilbury, C & Evans, H

Control of Asian cycad scale on *Cycas revoluta* and *C. taitungensis* using Imicide trunk microinjection: Tattar, TA & Farran, A

Multiyear evaluation of mating disruption treatments against gypsy moth: Tobin, PC; Thorpe, K & Blackburn, L

Bacillus thuringiensis toxins trigger receptor shedding from gypsy moth midgut cells: Valaitis, A

Evaluation of several neonicotiniods and delivery methods for EAB control: Wang, B; Mastro, V & Gao, R

Evaluation of non-native Tsuga species as replacements for *T. canadensis* killed by hemlock woolly adelgid: Weston, PA & Harper, RW

ATTENDEES

16th USDA INTERAGENCY RESEARCH FORUM ON GYPSY MOTH AND OTHER INVASIVE SPECIES

JANUARY 10-13, 2006
Annapolis, Maryland

Robert Acciavatti
USDA Forest Service, FHP
180 Canfield Street
Morgantown, WV 26505
racciavatti@fs.fed.us

Rob Ahern
University of Maryland
4112 Plant Sciences Bldg.
College Park, MD 20742
rga@umd.edu

Cora M. Allard
Clemson University
Entomology
114 Long Hall
Clemson, SC 29634
callara@clemson.edu

Clair A. Allen
Utah Dept. Agriculture
& Food
350 North Redwood Road
Salt Lake City, UT 84114
clairallen@utah.gov

Jaime Amirault
Maryland Dept. Agriculture
50 Harry S. Truman Pkwy.
Annapolis, MD 21401

Rich Anacker
Maryland Dept. Agriculture
50 Harry S. Truman Pkwy.
Annapolis, MD 21401
anackerRH@mda.state.md.us

Andrea Anulewicz
Michigan State University
11751 Cardwell St.
Livonia, MI 48150
agiusand@msu.edu

Chris Asaro
Virginia Dept. Forestry
900 Natural Resources Dr.
Charlottesville, VA 22903
chris.asaro@dof.virginia.gov

Allan Auclair
USDA APHIS, PPQ
4700 River Road
Riverdale, MD 20737
allan.auclair@aphis.usda.gov

Robert Baca
USDA APHIS
4700 River Road, Unit 150
Riverdale, MD 20737
Robert.M.Baca@aphis.usda.gov

John Baggett
Fairfax County FPM Section
12055 Government Center Pkwy.
Fairfax, VA 22035
John.Baggett@fairfaxcounty.gov

Thomas Baker
Pennsylvania State University
105 Chemical Ecology Lab.
University Park, PA 16802
tcb10@osu.edu

Yuri Baranchikov
VN Sukachev Institute of Forest
Akademgorodok
Krasnoyarsk, 660036, Russia
Baranchikov_Yuri@yahoo.com

Deborah Barber
The Nature Conservancy
5410 Grosvenor Lane
Bethesda, MD 20815
dbarber@tnc.org

Dick Bean
Maryland Dept. Agriculture
50 Harry S. Truman Pkwy.
Annapolis, MD 21401
beanra@mda.state.md.us

Robin Bedding
CSIRO Entomology
GPO Box 1700
Canberra ACT 2601, Australia
robin.bedding@csiro.au

Philip Bell
USDA, APHIS, PPQ
920 Main Campus Dr., Ste. 200
Raleigh, NC 27606
philip.d.bell@aphis.usda.gov

Susan Bentz
US National Arboretum
11601 Old Pond Drive
Glenn Dale, MD 20769
sbentz@ars-grin.gov

Ronald Blaskovich
USDA APHIA
325 Mercer Corporate Park
Robbinsville, NJ 08691
ronald.m.blaskovich@aphis.usda.gov

George Boettner
University of Massachusetts
250 Natural Resources Road
Amherst, MA 01003
boettner@psis.umass.edu

Tiffany Bogich
Pennsylvania State University
208 Mueller Lab
University Park, PA 16801
tlb927@psu.edu

Joyce Bolton
USDA ARS NAL
10301 Baltimore Avenue
Beltsville, MD 20705
jbolton@nal.usda.gov

Suzanne Bond
USDA APHIS
4700 River Road
Riverdale, MD 20737
suzanne.m.bond@aphis.usda.gov

Jerry Boughton
USDA Forest Service
11 Campus Blvd.
Newtown Square, PA 19073
jboughton@fs.fed.us

J. Robert Bridges
USDA Forest Service
11 Campus Blvd., Ste. 200
Newtown Square, PA 19073
rbridges@fs.fed.us

Susan A. Bright
USDA, APHIS, PPQ
4700 River Road, Unit 150
Riverdale, MD 20737
susan.a.bright@aphis.usda.gov

Kerry Britton
USDA Forest Service
1601 North Kent, RPF-7
Arlington, VA 22209
kbritton01@fs.fed.us

Jeff Brothers
Delaware Dept. Agriculture
2320 S. DuPont Highway
Dover, DE 19901
Jeffrey.Brothers@state.de.us

Beth Buchanan
Davey Resource Group
1500 N. Manuta St., Box 5193
Kent, OH 44240
bbuchanan@davey.com

Rose Buckner
Maryland Dept. Agriculture
50 Harry S. Truman Pkwy.
Annapolis, MD 21401
bucknerm@mda.state.md.us

Stephen Bullington
USDA APHIS, PPQ
401 E.Louther St., Ste. 102
Carlisle, PA 17013
Stephen.W.Bullington@aphis.usda.gov

Russ Bulluck
USDA APHIS
1730 Varsity Dr., Ste. 400
Raleigh, NC 27529
Russ.Bulluck@aphis.usda.gov

Leon Bunce
USDA APHIS
920 Main Campus Dr., Ste. 200
Raleigh, NC 27606
Leon.K.Bunce@aphis.usda.gov

Layla Burgess
Clemson University
114 Long Hall
Clemson, SC 29634
laylab@clemson.edu

Charlie Burnham
Massachusetts Dept. of
Conservation
P.O. Box 484
Amherst, MA 01004
Charlie.Burnham@state.ma.us

Filipinas Caliboso
Prince William Co.–Gypsy Moth
4092 Merchant Plaza, Ste. A
Woodbridge, VA 22192

E. Alan Cameron
Pennsylvania State University
541 McCormick Avenue
State College, PA 16801
eajabaka@adelphia.net

Scott Cameron
International Paper
719 Southlands Road
Bainbridge, GA 39819
scott.cameron@ipaper.com

Faith Campbell
The Nature Conservancy
4245 North Fairfax Drive
Arlington, VA 22203
phytodoer@aol.com

Sally Cannon
Maryland Dept. Agriculture
P.O. Box 178
Cheltenham, MD 20623
southernfpm@erols.com

Angus Carnegie
NSW Dept. Primary Industries
201 Elizabeth Street
Beecroft NSW 2119, Australia
angusc@sf.nsw.gov.au

Jean-Guy Champagne
Canadian Food Inspection
Agency
2001 University St., Rm. 746-D
Montréal (QC) H3A 3N2
champagnejg@inspection.gc.ca

Randolph Ciurlino
Delaware Dept. Agriculture
2320 S. DuPont Highway
Dover, DE 19901
Randolph.Ciurlino@state.de.us

David Clement
University of Maryland, Coop.
Ext.12005 Homewood Road
Ellicott City, MD 21042
clement@umd.edu

Dave Cohen
Maryland Dept. Agriculture
50 Harry S. Truman Pkwy.
Annapolis, MD 21401
mdafpm@hereintown.net

Jason Cole
Helicopter Applicators, Inc.
1670 York Rd.
Gettysburg, PA 17325
jcole@helicopterapplicators.com

Reg Coler
ISCA Technologies, Inc.
2060 Chicago Ave., #C-2
Riverside, CA 92507
ISCA@ISCATech.com

Robert Coulson
Texas A&M University
Dept. Entomology
HEEP Center, Room 408
College Station, TX 77843
r-coulson@tamu.edu

Damon Crook
USDA APHIS
Bldg. 1398
Otis ANGB, MA 02542
damon.j.crook@aphis.usda.gov

Don Dagnan
USDA Forest Service
11 Campus Blvd.
Newtown Square, PA 19073
dcdagnan@fs.fed.us

Vince D'Amico, III
USDA Forest Service
c/o University of Delaware
Newark, DE 19717
vdamico@elbowfarm.com

Peter deGroot
Canadian Forest Service
1219 Queen Street
Sault Ste. Marie, Ontario
pdegroot@nrcan.gc.ca

Thomas Denholm
NJ Dept. Agriculture
Box 330
Trenton, NJ 08625
tom.denholm@ag.state.nj.us

Don Diamond
JJ Mauget Co.
5435 Peck Road
Arcadia, CA 91006
mary@mauget.com

Andrea Diss-Torrance
Wisconsin Dept. Nat. Resources
1101 Lawrence St.
Madison, WI 53715
andrea.diss@dnr.state.wi.us

Joseph Doccola
Arborjet, Inc.
70B Cross Street
Winchester, MA 01890
joedoccola@arborjet.com

Mary Ellen Dix
USDA Forest Service
1601 North Kent St.
Arlington, VA 22209
mdix@fs.fed.us

Kevin Dodds
USDA Forest Service
271 Mast Road
Durham, NH 03824
kdodds@fs.fed.us

Nathan Dodds
JJ Mauget Co.
5435 Peck Road
Arcadia, CA 91006
mary@mauget.com

G. Keith Douce
University of Georgia
4601 Research Way
Tifton, GA 31793
kdouce@uga.edu

Marla Downing
USDA Forest Service
2150 Centre Ave., Bldg. A,
Ste. 331
Fort Collins, CO 80526
mdowning@fs.fed.us

Adrian Duehl
North Carolina State University
Entomology, Box 7626
Raleigh, NC 27695
ajduehl@ncsu.edu

Don Duerr
USDA Forest Service
1720 Peachtree Rd. NW
Atlanta, GA 30309
dduerr@fs.fed.us

Todd Edgerton
Virginia Dept. Forestry
900 Natural Resources Dr.
Ste. 800
Charlottesville, VA 22903
todd.edgerton@dof.virginia.gov

Joseph Elkinton
University of Massachusetts
Fernald Hall
Amherst, MA 01003
Elkinton@ent.umass.edu

Jodie Ellis
Purdue University, Smith Hall
901 W. State Street
West Lafayette, IN 47907
ellisj@purdue.edu

Roeland Elliston
USDA APHIS, PPQ
2150 Centre Avenue
Ft. Collins, CO 80526
roeland.j.Elliston@aphis.usda.gov

Barry Emens
USDA, APHIS, PPQ
P.O. Box 330
Trenton, NJ 08625
barry.c.emens@aphis.usda.gov

Nadir Erbilgin
University of California-Berkeley
140 Mulford Hall
Berkeley, CA 94704
erbilgin@nature.berkeley.edu

Hugh Evans
Forest Research,
Alice Holt Lodge
Wrecclesham, Farnham, Surrey
GU10 4LH United Kingdom
hugh.evans@forestry.gov.uk

Lynn Evans-Goldner
USDA APHIS
4700 River Road
Riverdale, MD 20737
lynn.e.goldner@aphis.usda.gov

Richard Feeney
Maryland Dept. Agriculture
50 Harry S. Truman Pkwy.
Annapolis, MD 21401

Claudia Ferguson
USDA APHIS, PPQ
201 Varick Street, Rm. 904
New York, NY 10014
Claudia.Ferguson@aphis.usda.gov

Frank Finch
Fairfax County FPM Section
12055 Government Center Pkwy.
Fairfax, VA 22035
frank.finch@fairfaxcounty.gov

Richard Fine
USDA APHIS, PPQ
325 Corporate Blvd.
Robbinsville, NJ 08691
richard.r.fine@aphis.usda.gov

Joel Floyd
USDA APHIS, PPQ
4700 River Road, Unit 137
Riverdale, MD 20737
joel.p.floyd@aphis.usda.gov

Joe Francese
USDA APHIS
Bldg. 1398
Otis ANGB, MA 02542
joe.francese@aphis.usda.gov

Michelle Frank
USDA Forest Service
11 Campus Blvd.
Newtown Square, PA 19073
mfrank@fs.fed.us

Ivich Fraser
USDA, APHIS, PPQ
5936 Ford Ct., Ste. 200
Brighton, MI 48116
ivich.fraser@aphis.usda.gov

Stephen Fraedrich
USDA Forest Service
320 Green Street
Athens, GA 30605
sfraedrich@fs.fed.us

Roger W. Fuester
USDA-ARS, BIIRL
501 S. Chapel Street
Newark, DE 19713
roger.fuester@ars.usda.gov

Weyman Fussell
USDA APHIS, PPQ
4700 Rive Road
Riverdale, MD 20737
weyman.fussell@aphis.usda.gov

Phillip Garcia
USDA APHIS
2150 Centre Ave., Bldg. B, 3E10
Fort Collins, CO 80526
phillip.e.garcia@aphis.usda.gov

Bruce Gill
Canadian Food Inspection Agency
960 Carling Ave., K.W.
Neatby Bldg.
Ottawa, Ontario K1A 0C6
gillbd@inspection.gc.ca

Nancy Gillette
USDA Forest Service
P.O. Box 245
Berkeley, CA 94701
ngillette@fs.fed.us

Joseph Gittleman
USDA APHIS, PPQ
320-01 Merrick Rd.
Amityville, NY 11701
joe.p.gittelman@aphis.usda.gov

Ken Gooch
Massachusetts Dept. Conserv./Rec.
740 South St., PO Box 1433
Pittsfield, MA 01202
ken.gooch@state.ma.us

Gordon Gordh
USDA APHIS
1730 Varsity Dr., Ste. 400
Raleigh, NC 27606
gordon.gordh@aphis.usda.gov

Kurt Gottschalk
USDA Forest Service
180 Canfield Street
Morgantown, WV 26505
kgottschalk@fs.fed.us

David Gray
Canadian Forest Service
P.O. Box 4000
Fredericton, NB, Canada E3B 5P7
dgray@nrcan.gc.ca

Sarah Green
Helicopter Applicators, Inc.
1670 York Road
Gettysburg, PA 17325
sgreen@helicopterapplicators.com

Matthew Greenstone
USDA ARS
BARC-West, Bldg. 011A
Beltsville, MD 20705
greenstm@ba.ars.usda.gov

Nina Grimaldi
Maryland Dept. Agriculture
50 Harry S. Truman Pkwy.
Annapolis, MD 21401
ngc1@att.net

Dawn Gunderson-Rindal
USDA ARS
BARC-West, Bldg. 011A
Beltsville, MD 20705
gundersd@ba.ars.usda.gov

Filadelfo Guzman
USDA ARS
10300 Baltimore Ave., Bldg. 007
Beltsville, MD 20705
guzmanf@ba.ars.usda.gov

Kevin Hackett
USDA ARS, National Program Staff
5601 Sunnyside Avenue
Beltsville, MD 20705
kjh@ars.usda.gov

Fred Hain
North Carolina State University
Box 7626, Grinnells Lab.
Raleigh, NC 27695
fred_hain@ncsu.edu

Ann Hajek
Department of Entomology
Cornell University
Ithaca, NY 14853
aeh4@cornell.edu

Betsie Handley
Maryland Dept. Agriculture
50 Harry S. Truman Pkwy.
Annapolis, MD 21401
mdacent@erols.com

Larry Hanks
Illinois Natural History Survey
505 S. Goodwin Ave.,
320 Morrill
Urbana, IL 61801
hanks@life.uiuc.edu

Heidi Hanlon
Cape May National Wildlife
Refuge
24 Kimbles Beach Rd.
Cape May Court House, NJ
08210
heidi_hanlon@fws.gov

Jim Hanula
USDA Forest Service
320 Green Street
Athens, GA 30602
jhanula@fs.fed.us

Dennis Haugen
USDA Forest Service
1992 Folwell Avenue
St. Paul, MN 55108
dhaugen@fs.fed.us

Nathan Havill
Yale University
Dept. Ecology & Evolutionary
Biol., New Haven, CT 06520
nathan.havill@yale.edu

Franck Herard
USDA ARS, EBCL
CS90013 Montferrier-sur-Lez,
34988, Saint-Gely-du-Fesc
Cedex, France
fherard@ars-ebcl.org

Robert Heyd
Michigan Dept. Natural
Resources, 1990 US 41 South
Marquette, MI 49855
Heydr@michigan.gov

Shelley Hicks
Maryland Department of
Agriculture
50 Harry S. Truman Pkwy.
Annapolis, MD 21401

Yasutomo Higashiura
Hokkaido Forest Research Inst.
Bibai, Hokkaido
079-0198 Japan
yasu@fri.bibai.hokaido.jp

Shivenand Hiremath
USDA Forest Service
359 Main Road
Delaware, OH 43015
shiremath@fs.fed.us

E. Richard Hoebeke
Dept. Entomology,
Comstock Hall
Cornell University
Ithaca, NY 14853
erh2@cornell.edu

Carol Holko
Maryland Department of
Agriculture
50 Harry S. Truman Pkwy.
Annapolis, MD 21401
HolkoCA@mda.state.md.us

Terrence Holton
GFS Chemicals, Inc.
867 McKinley Ave.
Columbus, OH 43222
terry@gfschemicals.com

Gregory Hoover
Dept. Entomology, 543 ASI Bldg.
Pennsylvania State University
University Park, PA 16802
gah10@psu.edu

Judy Hough-Goldstein
University of Delaware
531 S. College Avenue
Newark, DE 19716
jhough@udel.edu

Leland Humble
Canadian Forest Service, NRC
506 W. Burnside Road
Victoria, British Columbia
V8Z 1M5
lhumble@pfc.forestry.ca

Edson Tadeu Iede
EMBRAPA
Estrada da Ribeira KM 111
83.411.000 Colombo-Parana, Brazil
iedeet@cnpf.embrapa.br

Kathleen JR Johnson
Oregon Dept. Agriculture
635 Capitol St., NE
Salem, OR 97301
kjohnson@oda.state.or.us

Bill Kauffman
USDA APHIS
2150 Centre Ave., Bldg. B 3E10
Fort Collins, CO 80526
William.c.kauffman@aphis.usda.gov

Melody Keena
USDA Forest Service
51 Mill Pond Rd.
Hamden, CT 06514
mkeena@fs.fed.us

Craig Kellogg
USDA APHIS, PPQ
5936 Ford Ct., Ste. 200
Brighton, MI 48116
craig.kellogg@aphis.usda.gov

Ashot Khrimian
USDA ARS, 10300 Baltimore
Ave., Bldg. 007
Beltsville, MD 20705
khrimiaa@ba.ars.usda.gov

Kathleen Kidd
NC Dept. Agriculture
1060 Mail Service Center
Raleigh, NC 27699
kathleen.kidd@ncmail.net

Troy Kimoto
Canadian Food Inspection
Agency, 4321 Still Creek Dr.,
Fl. 4, Rm. 400, Burnaby.
British Columbia V5C 6S7
kimotot@inspection.gc.ca

Karen Kish
West Virginia Dept. Agriculture
1900 Kanawha Blvd.
Charleston, WV 25305
kkish@ag.state.wv.us

Carolyn Klass
Cornell University
4140 Comstock Hall
Ithaca, NY 14853
ck20@cornell.edu

Suzanne Klick
University of Maryland
11975 Homewood Road
Ellicott City, MD 21042
sklick@umd.edu

Brian Kopper
USDA APHIS
920 Main Campus Dr.
Raleigh, NC 27606
brian.j.kopper@aphis.usda.gov

John Kough
US EPA
1200 Pennsylvania Ave.
Washington, DC 20460
kough.john@epa.gov

Stephanie Kubilus
USDA APHIS
4700 River Road
Riverdale, MD 20737
stephanie.jubilus@aphis.usda.gov

Dan Kucera
337 Staghorn Way
West Chester, PA 19380

Craig Kuhn
Maryland Dept. Agriculture
P.O. Box 502
Forest Hill, MD 21050
nefpm@hotmail.com

Peter Kuntz
Kuntz Forestry Consulting
225 Sunray Rd.
Oakville, Ontario L6L 3R7
pkrpf@sympatico.ca

Kerrie Kyde
Maryland Dept. Natural
Resources, 580 Taylor Avenue,
E-1, Annapolis, MD 21401
kkyde@dnr@state.md.us

James LaBonte
Oregon Dept. Agriculture
635 Capitol St., NE
Salem, OR 97301
jlabonte@oda.state.or.us

Ashley Lamb
Virginia Tech
216 Price Hall, Entomology
Blacksburg, VA 24061
aslamb@vt.edu

David Lance
USDA, APHIS, PPQ
Bldg. 1398
Otis ANGB, MA 02542
david.r.lance@aphis.usda.gov

Charles Layton
Fairfax County Forest Pest Prg.
12055 Government Center Pkwy.
Fairfax, VA 22035
charles.Layton@fairfaxcounty.gov

James Lazell
The Conservation Agency
1140 Monroe St.
Jackson, MS 39202
HQ@theconservationagency.org

Danny Lee
USDA Forest Service
P.O. Box 268D
Asheville, NC 28802
dclee@fs.fed.us

Donna Leonard
USDA Forest Service, FHP
200 WT Weaver Blvd.
Asheville, NC 28802
dleonard@fs.fed.us

Phil Lewis
USDA APHIS, PPQ
Bldg. 1398
Otis ANGB, MA 02542
philip.a.lewis@aphis.usda.gov

Andrew Liebhold
USDA Forest Service
180 Canfield Street
Morgantown, WV 26505
aliebhold@fs.fed.us

Andreas Linde
University of Applied Sciences
Alfred-Moeller Str. 26
Eberswalde, 16225, Germany
alinde@fh-eberswade.de

Houping Liu
Michigan State University
243 Natural Science Bldg.
East Lansing, MI 48823
liuho@msu.edu

Jesse Logan
USDA Forest Service
860 N. 1200 East
Logan, UT 84321
jalogan@fs.fed.us

Wenhua Lu
University of Massachusetts
c/o 1140 Monroe St.
Jackson, MS 39202
wenhua@psis.umass.edu

Ann Lynch
USDA Forest Service
2500 South Pine Knoll
Flagstaff, AZ 86001
alynch@fs.fed.us

Bonnie MacCulloch
99 North College Ave.
Newark, DE 19711
bmacculloch@gmail.com

Martin MacKenzie
USDA Forest Service
180 Canfield Street
Morgantown, WV 26505
mmackenzie@fs.fed.us

Priscilla MacLean
Hercon Environmental
P.O. Box 435, Emigsville, PA 17318
pmaclean@herconenviorn.com

Joan Mahoney
NY State Dept. Agric. & Markets
24 Ventura Dr.
N. Babylon, NY 11703
joan.mahoney@agmkt.state.ny.us

Stephen Malan
Maryland Dept. Agriculture
50 Harry S. Truman Pkwy.
Annapolis, MD 21401
malansc@mda.state.md.us

Mary Kay Malinoski
Maryland Coop. Ext. Svc.
12005 Homewood Road
Ellicott City, MD 21042
mkmal@umd.edu

Robert Mangold
USDA Forest Service
1601 North Kent, RPC-7
Arlington, VA 22209
rmangold@fs.fed.us

Rick Manning
TruGreen Chemlawn
1275 Davis Road, Ste. 240
Elgin, IL 60123
rickmanning@trugreenmail.com

Tim Marasco
Pennsylvania Bureau of Forestry
208 Airport Drive
Middletown, PA 17057
tmarasco@state.pa.us

Ken Marchant
Canadian Food Inspection Agency
174 Stone Road West
Guelph, Ontario N1G 4S9
marchantk@inspection.gc.ca

Christine Markham
USDA APHIS, PPQ
920 Main Campus Dr., Ste. 200
Raleigh, NC 27606
christine.markham@aphis.usda.gov

James Marra
WA State Dept. Agriculture
3939 Cleveland Ave. SE
Olympia, WA 98501
jmarra@agr.wa.gov

Philip Marshall
Indiana Division of Forestry
2782 W. County Rd. 540 S
Vallonia, IN 47281
pmarshall@hsonline.net

Debra Martin
Virginia Dept. Agric. & Cons. Aff.
P.O. Box 1163
Richmond, VA 23218
Debra.Martin@vdacs.Virginia.gov

Victor C. Mastro
USDA, APHIS, PPQ
Bldg. 1398
Otis ANGB, MA 02542
vic.mastro@aphis.usda.gov

David Mausel
Virginia Tech
216A Price Hall, MC 0319
Blacksburg, VA 24016
dmausel@vt.edu

Tom McAvoy
Virginia Tech
216A Price Hall, MC 0319
Blacksburg, VA 24016
tmcavoy@vt.edu

Sally McElwey
USDA Forest Service
240 W. Prospect
Fort Collins, CO 80525
sjmcelwey@fs.fed.us

Max W. McFadden
The Heron Group, LLC
P.O. Box 741
Georgetown, DE 19947
mcfadden@dca.net

Michael McManus
USDA Forest Service
51 Mill Pond Road
Hamden, CT 06514
mlmcmanus@fs.fed.us

Deborah McPartlan
USDA APHIS
4700 River Road, Unit 137
Riverdale, MD 20737
Deborah.l.mcpartlan@usda.gov

Bruce Miller
The Heron Group, LLC
P.O. Box 406
North East, PA 16428
bjmiller@psu.edu

Michael Montgomery
USDA Forest Service
51 Mill Pond Road
Hamden, CT 06514
mmontgomery@fs.fed.us

Joe Mudd
Maryland Dept. Agriculture
50 Harry S. Truman Pkwy.
Annapolis, MD 21401

John Mueller
Fumigation Service & Supply Co.
16950 Westfield Park Rd.
Westfield, IN 46074
fumig8r@aol.com

Steve Munson
USDA Forest Service
4746 S. 1900 E.
Ogden, UT 84403
smunson@fs.fed.us

Kiesett Newton
USDA EPHIS
4700 River Road, Unit 130
Riverdale, MD 20737
kiesett.v.newton@aphis.usda.gov

Larry Nichols
Virginia Dept. Agriculture
P.O. Box 1163
Richmond, VA 23218
larry.nichols@vdacs.virginia.gov

Larry Norton
Bayer, 739 Blair Road
Bethlehem, PA 18017
larry.norton@bayercropscience.com

William Oldland
USDA Forest Service
180 Canfield Street
Morgantown, WV 26505
woldland@fs.fed.us

Brad Onken
USDA Forest Service
180 Canfield Street
Morgantown, WV 26505
bonken@fs.fed.us

Andrei Orlinski
EPPO
1, Rue le Nôtre
75016 Paris, France
orlinski@eppo.fr

Richard Orr
National Invasive Species Cncl.
1201 I Street NW
Washington, DC 20005
richard.orr@ios.doi.gov

Eric Ott
LSU Ag Center
342 Jennifer Jean Dr.
Baton Rouge, LA 70808
eott@agcenter.lsu.edu

Bill Panagakos
USDA APHIS
320 Merrick Rd.
Amityville, NY 11701
william.s.panagakos@aphis.usda.gov

Annie Paradis
University of Massachusetts
101 Fernald Hall
Amherst, MA 01003
aparadis@psis.umass.edu

Gregory Parra
USDA APHIS
1730 University Drive, Ste. 400
Raleigh, NC 27606
greg.r.parra@aphis.usda.gov

Randall Peiffer
Delaware State University
1200 DuPont Highway
Dover, DE 19901
rpeiffer@desu.edu

John Podgwaite
USDA Forest Service
51 Mill Pond Road
Hamden, CT 06514
jpodgwaite@fs.fed.us

Evan Preisser
University of Massachusetts
250 Natural Resources Rd.
Amherst, MA 01003
preisser@psis.umass.edu

Derek Puckett
USDA Forest Service
200 WT Weaver Blvd.
Asheville, NC 28804
dlpuckett@fs.fed.us

Robert Rabaglia
USDA Forest Service
1601 N. Kent St., RPC-7
Arlington, VA 22209
brabaglia@fs.fed.us

Iral Ragenovich
USDA Forest Service
P.O. Box 3623
Portland, OR 97208
iragenovich@fs.fed.us

Michael Raupp
University of Maryland
Department of Entomology
College Park, MS 20742
mraupp@umd.edu

Ken Rauscher
Michigan Dept. Agriculture
P.O. Box 30017
Lansing, MI 48933
rauscherk@michigan.gov

Richard Reardon
USDA Forest Service, FHTET
180 Canfield Street
Morgantown, WV 26505
rreardon@fs.fed.us

Yvette Redler
USDA APHIS
650 Capitol Mall, Ste. 6-200
Sacramento, CA 95814
yvette.j.redler@aphis.usda.gov

Laurie Reid
South Carolina Forestry
Commission
5500 Broad River Road
Columbia, SC 29210
lreid@forestry.state.sc.us

James Reilly
Dept. Entomology
Cornell University, Comstock Hall
Ithaca, NY 14853
jrr28@cornell.edu

James Rhea
USDA Forest Service
200 W.T. Weaver Blvd.
Asheville, NC 28804
rrhea@fs.fed.us

Kim Rice
Maryland Dept. Agriculture
50 Harry S. Truman Pkwy.
Annapolis, MD 21401
riceka@mda.state.md.us

Scott Roberts
TruGreen Chemlawn
1275 Davis Road, Ste. 240
Elgin, IL 60123
scottroberts@trugreenmail.com

Donald Rogers
NC Division of Forest Resources
1616 Mail Service Center
Raleigh,NC 27699
don.rogers@ncmail.net

Jim Rollins
Mauget
5435 Peck Road
Aracadia, CA 91006
mary@mauget.com

Alain Roques
INRA
Zoologie Forestière, BP 20619
Ardon 45166 Olivet, France
Alain.roques@orleans.inra.fr

Scott Salom
Virginia Tech
216 Price Hall., Dept. Entomology
Blacksburg, VA 24061
salom@vt.edu

Laura Samson
Alphawood Foundation
2451 N. Lincoln Ave., #205
Chicago, IL 60614
lsamson@alphawoodfoundation.org

Frank Sapio
USDA Forest Service
2150 Centre Ave., Bld. A, Ste. 331
Ft. Collins, CO 80526
fsapio@fs.fed.us

Al Sawyer
USDA, APHIS, PPQ
Bldg. 1398
Otis ANGB, MA 02542
alan.j.sawyer@aphis.usda.gov

Taylor Scarr
Ministry of Natural Resources
70 Foster Drive, Ste. 400
Sault Ste. Marie, Ontario P6A 6V5
taylor.scar@mnr.gov.on.ca

Paul Schaefer
USDA, ARS, BIIRL
501 S. Chapel St.
Newark, DE 19713
paulschaefer60@hotmail.com

Noel Schneeberger
USDA Forest Service
11 Campus Blvd., Ste. 200
Newtown Square, PA 19073
nschneeberger@fs.fed.us

Patricia Sellers
USDA Forest Service
401 Oakwood Drive
Harrisonburg, VA 220801
psellers@fs.fed.us

Gwen Servies
USDA APHIS PPQ
3920 North Rockwell
Chicago, IL 60618
gwen.servies@aphis.usda.gov

Ryan Shanley
Cornell University
Dept. Entomology, Comstock
Hall, Ithaca, NY 14853
rps33@cornell.edu

Troy Shaw
Fairfax County FPM Section
12055 Government Center Pkwy.
Fairfax, VA 22035
troy.shaw@fairfaxcounty.gov

Megan Sheremata
NY State Dept. Environ. Conserv.
47-40 21st St., 2nd Floor
Long Island City, NY 11101
mxsheremata@gw.dec.state.ny.us

Shigehiko Shiyake
Osaka Museum of Natural
History, Nagai Park
Osaka, Japan
shiyak@mus-nh.city.osaka.jp

Laura Shifflett
Frederick Co. Virginia Gov.
1805 Back Mountain Rd.
Winchester, VA 22602
lshiffle@co.frederick.va.us

Nathan Siegert
Michigan State University
243 Natural Science Bldg.
East Lansing, MI 48824
siegert1@msu.edu

Michael Simon
USDA APHIS
4700 River Road, Unit 60
Riverdale, MD 20737
michael.simon@aphis.usda.gov

James Slavicek
USDA, Forest Service
359 Main Road
Delaware, OH 43015
jslavicek@fs.fed.us

Bryan Smalley
Timber Products Services
P.O. Box 919
Conyers, GA 30012
bsmalley@tpinspection.com

Annemarie Smith
The Ohio State University
318 W. 12th St., 400 Aronoff Lab.
Columbus, OH 43210
smith.3746@osu.edu

Michael Smith
USDA ARS, BIIRL
501 S. Chapel Street
Newark, DE 19713
mtsmith@udel.edu

John Snitzer
Hood College
P.O.Box 38
Dickerson, MD 20842
navajuela@comcast.net

Lee Solter
Illinois Natural History Survey
1101 W. Peabody Dr., Box 18
Urbana, IL 61801
lsolter@uiuc.edu

Dennis Souto
USDA Forest Service
271 Mast Road
Durham, NH 03824
dsouto@fs.fed.us

Sven-Erik Spichiger
PA Bureau of Forestry, DCNR
208 Airport Drive, 2nd Floor
Middletown, PA 17057
sspichiger@state.pa.us

Mike Stefan
USDA APHIS, PPQ
4700 River Road
Riverdale, MD 20737
michael.b.stefan@usda.gov

Jéan Pierre Steffen
USDA OIG, Rm 410E Whitten Bldg.
1400 Independence Ave. SW
Washington, DC 20250
jpsteffen@oig.usda.gov

DeAnna Steiger
University of Delaware
246 Townsend Hall
Newark, DE 19716

John Stein
USDA Forest Service
180 Canfield Street
Morgantown, WV 26505
jstein@fs.fed.us

James Stimmel
Bureau of Plant Industries
2301 N. Cameron Street
Harrisburg, PA 17110
jstimmel@state.pa.us

John Strazanac
West Virginia University
Ag. Sci. Bldg., Evansdale Dr.
Morgantown, WV 26506
jstrazan@wvu.edu

Brian Sullivan
USDA Forest Service
2500 Shreveport Highway
Pineville, LA 71360
briansullivan@fs.fed.us

Jil Swearingen
National Park Service
4598 MacArthur Blvd. NW
Washington, DC 20007
jil_swearingen@nps.gov

Jon Sweeney
Canadian Forest Service
29 Sprucewood Dr.
New Maryland NB, Canada
E3C 1C6
jsweeney@nrcan.gc.ca

Bob Tatman
Maryland Dept. of Agriculture
50 Harry S. Truman Pkwy.
Annapolis, MD 21401
nefpm@erols.com

Terry Tattar
Mauget
5435 Peck Rd.
Arcadia, CA 91006
mary@mauget.com

Mark Taylor
Maryland Dept. of Agriculture
50 Harry S. Truman Pkwy.
Annapolis, MD 21401
taylormc@mda.state.md.us

Philip Taylor
USDA ARS
501 S. Chapel St.
Newark, DE 19713
philip.taylor@ars.usda.gov

Ksenia Tcheslavskaia
Dept. Entomology
Virginia Tech
Blacksburg, VA 24061
ktchesla@vt.edu

Steve Teale
State University of New York
Environmental Science & Forestry
Syracuse, NY 13210
sateale@esf.edu

Kevin Thorpe
USDA, ARS, BARC-West
10300 Baltimore Ave.
Beltsville, MD 20705
Thorpe@ba.ars.usda.gov

Robert Tichenor
Maryland Dept. Agriculture
50 Harry S. Truman Pkwy.
Annapolis, MD 21401
tichenrh@mda.state.md.us

Steve Tilley
Maryland Dept. of Agriculture
50 Harry S. Truman Pkwy.
Annapolis, MD 21401
fpmes@ccisp.net

Patrick Tobin
USDA Forest Service
180 Canfield Street
Morgantown, WV 26505
ptobin@fs.fed.us

Matthew Travis
Maryland Dept. Agriculture
50 Harry S. Truman Pkwy.
Annapolis, MD 21401
travisma@mda.state.md.us

R. Talbot Trotter
USDA Forest Service
51 Mill Pond Road
Hamden, CT 06514
rttrotter@fs.fed.us

Robert Trumbule
Maryland Dept. of Agriculture
6701 Lafayette Ave.
Riverdale, MD 20737
rtrumbule@erols.com

Richard Turcotte
USDA Forest Service
180 Canfield Street
Morgantown, WV 26505
rturcotte@fs.fed.us

Julie Twardowski
USDA APHIS
4700 River Road, Unit 137
Riverdale, MD 20737
julie.s.twardowski@aphis.usda.gov

Algimantas Valaitis
USDA Forest Service
359 Main Road
Delaware, OH 43015
avalaitis@fs.fed.us

John Vandenberg
USDA ARS
Tower Road
Ithaca, NY 14853
jdv3@cornell.edu

Roy VanDriesche
University of Massachusetts
Fernald Hall, Entomology
Amherst, MA 01003
vandries@nre.umass.edu

Philip van Wassenaer
Ontario Urban Forest Council
544 Exburg Crescent
Mississauga, Ontario L5G 2P4
pwassenaer1022@rogers.com

Kelly Veatch
TruGreen Chemlawn
1275 Davis Road, Ste. 240
Elgin, IL 60123
kellyveatch@trugreenmail.com

Shannon Wadkins
University of Maryland
11975 Homewood Rd.
Ellicott City, MD 21042

Karen Walker
Prince William County
4092 Merchant Plaza, Ste. A
Woodbridge, VA 22192
kwalker@pwcgov.org

Patsy Waszak
USDA, APHIS
930 Main Campus Dr., Ste. 200
Raleigh, NC 27606
patricia.a.waszak@aphis.usda.gov

Ralph Webb
USDA ARS, Bldg 007, Rm. 301
10300 Baltimore Ave.
Beltsville, MD 20705
webbr@ba.ars.usda.gov

Shahla Werner
PA Bureau of Forestry, DCNR
208 Airport Drive, 2nd Floor
Middletown, PA 17057-5027
shawerner@state.pa.us

Paul Weston
Cornell University
150 Insectary
Ithaca, NY 14853
paw23@cornell.edu

Geoffrey White
USDA ARS, Bldg. 007, Rm. 301
10300 Baltimore Avenue
Beltsville, MD 20705
whiteg@ba.ars.usda.gov

Brenda Whited
University of Massachusetts
250 Natural Resources Rd.
Amherst, MA 01003
bmw@nsm.umass.edu

Stefanie Whitmire
University of Puerto Rico
Dept. Agronomy & Soils
Mayagüez, PR 00623
swhitmire@uprm.edu

Jacob Wickham
SUNY, CESF, 241 Illick Hall
1 Forestry Drive
Syracuse, NY 13210
jdwickha@syr.edu

David Williams
USDA APHIS, PPQ
Bldg. 1398
Otis ANGB, MA 02542
david.w.wlliams@aphis.usda.gov

Richard Wilson
Ontario Ministry of
Natural Resources
70 Foster Drive, Ste. 400
Sault Ste. Marie, Ontario P6A 6V5
richard.wilson@mnr.gov.on.ca

Gloria Witkus
University of Massachusetts
250 Natural Resources Rd.
Amherst, MA 01003
gwitkus@psis.umass.edu

Jim Writer
USDA APHIS, PPQ
4700 River Road, Unit 150
Riverdale, MD 20737
james.v.writer@aphis.usda.gov

Gottschalk, Kurt W., ed. 2007. **Proceedings, 17th U.S.
    Department of Agriculture interagency research forum on
    gypsy moth and other invasive species 2006**; 2006 January
    10-13; Annapolis, MD. Gen. Tech. Rep. NRS-P-10. Newtown
    Square, PA: U.S. Department of Agriculture, Forest Service,
    Northern Research Station. 117 p.

Contains three abstracts and papers from the 2005 Forum and 70
abstracts and papers of oral and poster presentations on gypsy
moth and other invasive species biology, molecular biology,
ecology, impacts, and management presented at the annual U. S.
Department of Agriculture Interagency Research Forum on Gypsy
Moth and Other Invasive Species.